# THRIVE IN YOUR COMPANY

## HILTON CATT AND PATRICIA SCUDAMORE

ORION BUSINESS
BOOKS

The right of Hilton Catt and Patricia Scudamore to
be identified as the authors of this work has been
asserted by them in accordance with the
Copyright, Designs and Patents Act 1988.

This edition published in Great Britain in 2000 by
Orion Business
An imprint of The Orion Publishing Group Ltd
Orion House,
5 Upper St Martin's Lane,
London WC2H 9EA

A CIP catalogue record for this book
is available from the British Library.

ISBN 1 84203 039 6

Typeset by Deltatype Ltd, Birkenhead
Printed and bound in Great Britain
by Clays Ltd, St Ives plc.

# CONTENTS

# INTRODUCTION

## WHAT YOU ARE GOING TO GET FROM THIS BOOK

*Thrive in Your Company* is a new look at making your company work for you and achieving your ambitions. It shows you how to build on those basic survive and win skills and come up trumps in increasingly difficult modern conditions. So, irrespective of the job you do or the kind of organisation you work for, if you are looking for a toolkit of practical up-to-the-minute ideas for steering clear of dead ends and moving yourself forward, there is something in here for you.

Among the topics we look at are:

- how to assess your company – can it deliver the kind of career you want?

- how to stop your company viewing you as part of the woodwork; how to make them see your potential

- how to boost your bargaining power with your company – do they attach the right value to your input?

- how to upgrade your image – is your face in the frame when good opportunities come up?

- how to negotiate a better deal for yourself; how to avoid the bogey of underachieving

- how to handle the move into top jobs –

are you ready to say yes when the big promotion chance comes your way?

- how to deal with the increasing number of small companies, flat companies and fragmented companies; how to create a career for yourself when you work in organisations such as these.

The examples and case studies we use in *Thrive in Your Company* are all drawn from real life. They illustrate what works and what doesn't in the kind of world we live in today. In common with other titles in the Orion *Career PowerTools* series, the lessons in *Thrive in Your Company* appear in the form of twenty golden rules that you will come across as you work your way through the book. These twenty golden rules are brought together and expanded on in the final part.

......................................................................

# QUICK QUIZ: CAN YOU SURVIVE AND WIN?

To begin with, here's a quick quiz to establish how sharp your survive and win skills are. Go through these ten questions and tick the answer that most closely matches the one that you would give. See what we have to say at the end.

### Question 1

Two years ago you had too much to drink at the office party and made a bit of a fool of yourself. The following day your boss had a few stern words to say to you about your behaviour and the relationship between the two of you has been distinctly icy ever since. You have now been passed by twice for promotion and there is no possible explanation other than the office party incident is still being held against you. Do you:

A: ☐ Confront the boss?

B: ☐ Go and see the managing director and complain about the way your boss is treating you?

C: ☐ Do nothing and hope that eventually your lapse will be forgotten?

D: ☐ Conclude that as far as your company is concerned there will always be a black mark against you and seek the opportunities you are looking for elsewhere?

E: ☐ Say you will resign if you are not offered the next promotion?

## Question 2

Your company acquires some new state-of-the-art technology and they ask you to take responsibility for it. Part of the deal is that you will receive training in the very latest techniques, but you are concerned when you hear that you won't receive any additional salary for your increased responsibilities. Do you?

A: ☐ Accept, taking the view that you will tackle the problem of your salary once you have got the skills and experience associated with the new technology under your belt?

B: ☐ Accept, making the point you are not happy with the salary?

C: ☐ Make an increase in your salary a condition of your acceptance?

D: ☐ Ask for a deal linking an increase in your salary with the acquisition of new technology skills, i.e. your increase will become payable at some point in the future?

E: ☐ Say you are not interested?

## Question 3

A job you would like is offered to an outside candidate. When you approach the personnel manager to find out why you were not considered the answer you get is that no one thought you would be interested. Do you?

A: ☐ Feel that the company has let you down and take this as a signal to put yourself on the outside job market?

B: ☐ Blame yourself and make sure you make a better job of communicating your aims next time?

C: ☐ Resign in protest?

D: ☐ Make a formal complaint against the personnel manager and ask for an apology in writing?

E: ☐ Give your company an ultimatum that you will be leaving them if they don't do better in future?

## Question 4

You are in a position where you know you can get a job offer from a competitor whenever you want to. You also know that you can inflict considerable damage on your company if you go to work for a competitor. You now want to negotiate an improvement in your pay and perks. Do you:

A: ☐ Make your case with no mention of what you would do if the company said no?

B: ☐ Get a job offer from a competitor and show it to your company at the same time that you put in your demands?

C: ☐ Get a job offer from the competitor, resign, then wait for your company to buy you off?

D: ☐ Make your case but at the same time warn your company that if you don't get what you are looking for you will start looking for another job?

E: ☐ State your case and give your company a solemn pledge that you won't go and work for a competitor – even if they say no?

## Question 5

A few weeks ago you asked your boss for a salary increase to take account of some new responsibilities you have taken on. Your boss said that he would have to discuss the matter with the managing director and get back to you. Now he has told you that the managing director has said no to your increase. Do you:

A: ☐ Confront the managing director yourself?

B: ☐ Tell your boss you are going to look for another job?

C: ☐ Put your arguments in writing and send copies to both your boss and the managing director?

D: ☐ Refuse to carry out the new responsibilities until you get your rise?

E: ☐ Take stock and decide whether to try again in six months. Decide at the same time whether you would gain anything from putting yourself on the outside job market?

## Question 6

You have been trying to get a job in your company's public relations office for some time but up to now you have had no joy at all. Indeed, when there are vacancies, your company seems to prefer people from outside. You have now been offered a good job in another part of the company – a job you would be happy to accept but for your ambition of getting into public relations. By saying no, however, you realise you will be running the risk of being written off as far as future promotions are concerned and you can't afford to do this because you are stagnating in your present role. Do you:

A: ☐ Accept the job you have been offered?

B: ☐ Accept with the proviso that you would still prefer a job in public relations?

C: ☐ Decline and hope for the best?

D: ☐ Decline and start applying for jobs in public relations with other companies?

E: ☐ Leave it to your boss to make the decision for you?

## Question 7

You are in a senior management position with a company where you have long service. The company recruits an external candidate at the same level as you and you find out, that this person is being paid a much higher salary. Do you:

A: ☐ Complain to the managing director immediately?

B:  ☐ Resign in protest?

C:  ☐ Enlist support among your fellow senior managers?

D:  ☐ Start looking for another job?

E:  ☐ Accept that people recruited on the outside job market command higher salaries?

## Question 8

You are promoted into a job which puts you at the very pinnacle of your profession but the pay rise you get is much less than you were expecting. Do you:

A:  ☐ Say nothing?

B:  ☐ Say nothing, but leave it for a few months then try to get your salary put right?

C:  ☐ Complain immediately?

D:  ☐ Look for another job?

E:  ☐ Decline the promotion on the grounds that the salary isn't adequate?

## Question 9

You work in a small company where, because of bonuses and commissions, you earn a very good salary. You are now looking for a promotion which your company cannot offer you because of its size. You are finding, however, that the promotion jobs you are applying for on the outside job market pay lower salaries than your current earnings. Do you:

A:  ☐ Read this as a signal to stay where you are?

B:  ☐ Try applying for jobs higher up the ladder even though you realise you will be overreaching?

C:  ☐ Wait two years and see if the situation changes?

D:  ☐ Accept that advancing your career sometimes means having to take a step backwards in earnings?

E:  ☐ See if a new company will compensate you for the loss of earnings?

## Question 10

You have been promoted into a highly responsible and well paid job but you then find that the pressures are too much for you. Do you:

A:  ☐ Keep silent and flog on?

B:  ☐ Resign immediately?

C:  ☐ Tell your company and try to come to an agreement with them on the way forward?

D:  ☐ Keep silent and look for another job?

E:  ☐ Ask your doctor to give you a sick note and leave the company to decide how to deal with your absence?

How did you get on? The answers we are looking for are:

| 1 – D | 2 – A | 3 – B | 4 – A | 5 – E |
| 6 – A | 7 – E | 8 – B | 9 – D | 10 – C |

If you didn't give these responses, read on. When you have finished reading this book, hopefully you will feel more able to answer in a way that will help you thrive in your company.

## Part one

# YOU AND YOUR JOB

**I**n terms of your career, what are you expecting from your company and, at the same time, are you being realistic?

In this part we will look at the kind of questions you need to ask yourself about your situation at work and your ambitions. We will be focusing on:

• how company cultures, structures and situations differ: how these differences affect you; how a winning strategy in one organisation could be flogging a dead horse in another

• seeing if your job is safe: knowing when you might be standing on the edge of a precipice

• seeing where you are going: checking you are not stagnating

• the advantages of realising your ambitions internally: the relative lack of risk compared with making moves on the outside job market

• introducing you to the concept of the self-managed career (these days it's you in charge, no one else)

• forgetting the moans and groans; instead, getting you to see your job as the best asset you've got and treating it accordingly

• seeing where you might be trying to go too far too fast or in directions that might be difficult: where it could be you to blame for your lack of success rather than your company

- avoiding ambitions that are too narrow; seeing, instead, the benefits of being flexible and opportunistic (the art of the possible)

- defining your aims – what you are looking to your company to provide.

..................................................................

# PROFILING YOUR COMPANY

What kind of company do you work for? Is it a big company, is it a small company, or is it somewhere in between? What is its attitude towards developing and promoting people? Does it have a policy of using home-grown talent or do the best jobs always go to out-siders?

The answers to these questions and a few more should tell us a great deal about your company's ability to provide you with the kind of future you are looking for but, to give some real life dimensions to corporate profil-ing, look at the following case study of three young business graduates.

### CASE STUDY: LAURA, MIKE AND ANDREA

Laura, Mike and Andrea are all in their mid to late twenties, all hard-working, all with their eyes on going places, but there the similarities end.

Laura works for a big multinational in a specialist corporate strategy unit. Her career plan is prede-termined: she will remain in her present post for a further year, at the end of which time she will be appointed to an operational management role. If at any point she feels unhappy about the way things are unfolding she has access to an in-house career counselling centre where help and guidance are always available.

Mike is also employed by a big multinational, except in his case the company is broken down into a number of separate businesses that all operate independently. There is a small head office but most authority is devolved. Mike's job is that of sales executive in one of the businesses – a position he has held since he left university. There is no career plan for him and his fear is that unless he takes some positive action, he will be doing the same job in twenty years' time. Because of the fragmented nature of Mike's company, promotions from one business to another are rare. Indeed it is usual for the existence of opportunities elsewhere in the group only to become known when they appear in ads in the newspaper.

Andrea's situation is different from the others. She works for a small provincial firm of stockbrokers where she has built up an impressive portfolio of clients. With bonuses and commissions, she earns good money and she gets on well with the partners (the owners of the business). Because of the size of the firm, Andrea realises the prospects for promotion are restricted. There could be the offer of a partnership at some point in the future, but Andrea isn't banking on this.

Putting value judgements to one side for the moment (like Laura's company is 'better' than Mike's – which doesn't help anyone, especially Mike) the point we want to pick up on from these examples is that, from company to company, situations differ enormously and you need to take account of this. In particular, any view you take of your career needs to be taken in the context of the company you work for and any strategy you employ to get what you want or to move your career in the direction you want it to go in needs to be similarly paired. For instance, if Mike wants promotion he faces a bigger task than Laura, whereas for Andrea no amount of clever footwork is going to alter the fact that she has probably hit the ceiling in her company.

Given the importance of viewing careers in their corporate context, then, what factors do you need to consider when drawing up a profile of your company? What attributes count when it comes to determining whether or not your company is going to be a good career provider? In doing this little exercise remember that you have the advantage of knowing your company well. Unlike assessing an outside company as a potential employer you won't have to dig round for the information you need. Most of it will be in your head.

## Size

Size *is* important, yes. A big company should be able to deliver more than a small company, but as we saw in Mike's case, this doesn't always follow. Conversely, some small companies can be excellent providers of quality careers.

Also on the subject of size is the question of what you use to measure it. Number of employees in the UK? Number of employees world-wide? Sales turnover? Or some fancy yardstick, like market share?

With the increasing number of small firms and the tendency these days for big firms to be decentralised, fragmented, hollowed out or flattened down, size is no longer a stand-alone factor. To get a better picture, run size alongside other considerations such as structure and culture.

## Structure

If you work in a big company it may be decentralised, like Mike's – meaning, in effect, that it's little different to a small or medium-sized company and should be viewed as such. The pyramid-shaped hierarchies that formed the structure of so many larger companies (and up which traditional career paths climbed) have been flattened down in a lot of cases, the result of successive delayerings (taking out levels of management for cost-cutting reasons). If you work in one of these so-called 'flat' organisations you need to take account of this. (We devote part of Part 5 to careers in flat companies.)

## Culture

Some companies pay heed to the people they employ that goes far beyond lip service. Like Laura's company they take a great interest in training and career development. Conversely some companies take the view that employees should be responsible for their own careers. Culture has a lot to do with the personalities in companies, particularly the principals'. Cultures also change.

CASE STUDY: NAOMI

'Imagine the stunned silence when in the middle of a management meeting our new chief executive told everyone that he viewed people as the least important of the company's assets. Whether he was just trying to appear macho is hard to say, but it certainly caused a few raised eyebrows. Time to start getting a few options open was the general opinion afterwards.'

## Management functions

We mention this because in recent years a significant number of companies have divested themselves of what they consider to be non-core functions. In some cases these functions have been outsourced (e.g. the pension department has been closed and pensions are now dealt with by an outside firm of pensions advisers), or they have been rolled up into the responsibilities of other managers. Sometimes the divesting has been partial, in the sense that the function has been scaled down from its previous level of importance (e.g. recruitment is no longer dealt with by the human resources department – individual managers do their own recruiting and as a consequence the human resources department has been halved in size). The point here is that if your ambitions happen to lie in human resources management or pensions administration or some other specialised area, you need to take account of how your company views the function.

## Performance

How your company is performing (its profit-ability and its performance against key measures such as market share) clearly determines to a very great extent how it is going to fare as a career provider. The most people-minded business in the world won't be able to do much for you if its markets are declining. Here, it is important to distinguish between short-term cyclical trends – the ups and downs that affect all companies – and real indicators of which way the company is going, e.g. decline due to product obsolescence or shifts in global markets.

## Job security

Clearly this links with performance: an unprofitable company by definition won't be able to offer good long-term career prospects. But with security performance isn't the only issue. For example, some companies are notoriously 'hire and fire'. They may be doing well from a trading point of view but they have little time for people they regard as poor performers – which could include people who simply require more training or people who have had the bad luck to be sick.

## Investment

To an extent, a company's ability to invest stems from its performance and vice versa. However, it is also a reflection of its top management: their risk-taking skills and confidence in the future. Poor investment means not just poor investment in people (training, development, salaries) but also poor investment in technology. The result for you is your skills won't be kept up to date and, in today's world, this will be very detrimental to you. Watch out.

## Personalities

No view of a company is complete without taking into account the key personalities. The principals, the top level of management, are clearly important as they determine nearly all the factors we have touched on so far. The company's culture and structure as well as its willingness to invest revolves around the actions of a small group of people (e.g. key members of the board). In some companies (and not just small companies) this power can reside in one individual – hence an assessment of his or her personality is an essential part of profiling. Another critical personality as far as you are concerned is that of your immediate boss. The commitment of your boss to you and your career (or lack of it) is something else you need to take into account.

## Politics

What factions are in evidence in your company (there are bound to be some)? What faction do you belong to and is it in ascendancy or decline? What factions could stand in your way as you strive to move forwards?

## Pay and perks

Not least in this list is where your company stands when it comes to paying good salaries and providing good employment packages. Needless to say pay and perks is a difficult area and making comparisons isn't easy. We will have a lot to say on this subject as we move through the book. Suffice is to point out at this stage that you need to take care before coming to any hard and fast conclusions about your company's performance on the pay and perks front.

## Anything else?

These issues are by no means the only ones. Depending on where your ambitions lie, your company's capacity to deliver the career you want could be influenced by all sorts of other factors. For example, if your ambition is to get your boss's job, your boss's age and career prospects immediately come into play.

The idea behind profiling is not to make value judgements such as 'I work for a good/bad company', but rather to view your job situation objectively so that you can:

- form a realistic view of whether your company can meet your aspirations, short term and long term
- check that any stratagems you decide to use are the right ones.

With value judgements it pays to remember:

- there is no such thing as the perfect company: all organisations have their

flaws, the only question is whether you
are seeing them or not
- 'good' companies don't necessarily rate as
good career providers. For example,
people tend to stay with 'good'
companies meaning there are fewer
opportunities arising from staff turnover.
The higher you go up the ladder, the
worse this clogging up of the career paths
gets.

Profiling is not a one-off exercise, but something you need to do at regular intervals – say,
every year (if you are subject to an annual staff
appraisal, just before your appraisal interview
is not a bad time). Companies change, and
sometimes quite dramatically – a new chief
executive arrives on the scene, your company
is restructured, salaries are put on ice ... all
sorts of things can happen which completely
alter the complexion of things. Also, your own
ideas and needs change over time and you
should allow for this.

......................................................................

## SEEING WHETHER YOUR AIMS ARE REALISABLE

From person to person aims vary quite widely.
Take for example, six people working in the
design office of a mechanical engineering
company:

CASE STUDY: GREG, JOE, JACKIE, NADIM,
STEPHANIE, ED

*Greg:* 'I want to see myself in a good management job in the next two years – either in design

or contracting. I have a salary of at least £30k in my sights.'

*Joe:* 'I am eighteen months off retirement. All I want is for the job to last long enough for me to pick up my pension.'

*Jackie:* 'I graduated last year and I have only been with the firm six months. What I need at this stage is experience and training. I am not sure whether I want to stay in design. I want to put off any big decisions about my career for at least two years.'

*Nadim:* 'I am on a temporary contract. I am hoping for a permanent job at the end of the year but I realise that whether I get one or not depends on the company's order book.'

*Stephanie:* 'I like the job I am doing. I have no wish to take on any responsibilities other than the ones I have already got.'

*Ed:* 'I am an electrical engineer and most of the design work I am doing is mechanical – which I view as a complete waste of my qualifications and experience. I keep asking for a move to the control systems division but no one seems to listen to me.'

The question all of these people have got to ask themselves is whether their aims are realisable. Realisable, that is, as far as this particular company is concerned – which brings us back to profiling and one of the reasons why we did it.

Given what the six people in the example know about their company, can it deliver what they want?

CASE STUDY: CONTINUED

First, *Greg*. He has got pretty big ambitions, but the company is in growth. It was founded in 1986 and its annual turnover has gone up from £5m to £15m in the last ten years. The directors are a dynamic 'hands-on' lot and their record for promoting people from within is excellent. The salary Greg has in mind is well within the range the company pays to its design and project managers so there is no obvious mismatch between Greg's ambitions and what the company can offer. The big question, of course, is whether Greg is good enough. Will he be ready for this promotion into a management job in the two years he has given himself, or is he trying to bite off more than he can chew?

Next *Joe* and *Nadim*: Joe wants another eighteen months' work and Nadim wants a permanent job. Again, given the company's track record, their ambitions would seem to be realisable – and the same goes for *Jackie* and *Stephanie*. Jackie should get her two years' experience and Stephanie should be able to plod on in the way she wants.

But what about *Ed*? The big problem for Ed is that the control systems division consists of two people who have both been with the company since it started. The work is mostly on development and tends to be fairly static in volume – hence the likelihood of a further member of staff being required is remote. Alarm bells, therefore, for Ed: in pursuing these aims in this company he is probably chasing the end of the rainbow. What should he do? Think again, certainly. Is there anywhere else in-house where the talents of an electrical engineer might fit in? If not, is there any scope for a bit of job creation (there's more on job creation in Part 5). Failing that, Ed might have to face up to the fact that, as far as this company is concerned, his aims are not realisable. The company's profile and what he wants don't gel.

---

| **GOLDEN RULE 1** |

Be realistic about what your company can offer.

---

Chasing aims that are unrealisable is a common career problem. Here are a few more examples.

## CASE STUDY: UNREALISABLE AIMS

**Terri-Ann** wants a bigger car. *Problem:* Terri-Ann is on a staff grade which has a specific model of car allocated to it. Giving in to Terri-Ann would cause her company all sorts of difficulties (everyone else on her grade would want a bigger company car too).

**Graeme** wants a day off a week to go to college. *Problem:* Graeme is a key job holder in a small company where the only person who can deputise when he is away is the managing director.

**Shelagh** wants a guarantee that she won't have to spend more than three weeks a year working away from home. *Problem:* Shelagh is a trainer for a major software house. The company's clients are all over Europe. Only a handful are within what could be viewed as daily commuting distance.

The interesting point about Terri-Ann, Graeme and Shelagh is that their aims *might* be realisable in a different company. For example, a small firm with fewer members of staff might have more flexibility to give Terri-

Ann the kind of car she wants. Conversely, a big firm where there are more people to provide cover might be able to accommodate Graeme's wishes. But if you are faced with the fact that pursuing a particular aim in your company has practically no chance of success, what do you then do about it?

The signal will already be flashing at you to start looking for another job. But, before you do, ask yourself two important questions:

- How important is what you are trying to achieve? For instance, how important is it to Terri-Ann that she has a bigger car?
- Have you considered all the alternatives? For instance, in Graeme's case, is the course he wants to do available as an evening class or on an open learning basis?

Changing companies should be your action of last resort. There are a number of reasons for this:

- Irrespective of how well you do your research, a change of company is always a step into the unknown. The real Terri-Ann did leave her company for a job which offered her a better car. The result? The car never materialised and she was redundant within three months. The moral to this tale is that the modern world of jobs can be a very treacherous place.

- In a world where redundancy lists are often decided on the basis of 'last in, first out', changing jobs automatically puts you in a more precarious position.

- Leaving your company means leaving

behind any good work you have done to advance your career internally. In other words, you will be putting yourself back to square one. You will have to prove yourself all over again.

- Most occupational pension schemes are structured to benefit members who stick the course and go through to normal retiring age. In terms of frozen pensions and transfer values, people who leave get comparatively rough deals. Obviously the older you are, the more this is going to matter to you.

- If you have share options or bonuses which are collectable at some future date, you may find you lose all or part of them if you leave. Perks like these are not known as 'golden handcuffs' for nothing.

- Employers view people with too many voluntary job moves on their cvs with suspicion. They will be seen as people who can't fit in or who can't settle down and, with the accent very much on team-working these days, this won't get them very far. Put it this way, the number of voluntary job moves you can make without blotting your copybook is restricted. Put it another way, your job moves have got to count.

None of this is said to make you feel afraid of changing employer. In some circumstances it will be the right thing to do. The messages are simply these:

- don't change jobs for trivial or unnecessary reasons; save your moves for when it matters

- it is much better for you if you can achieve your aims internally.

There is an important last point to consider here: your assessment of your company could be wrong. It could have the capacity to deliver what you want but, for all sorts of possible reasons, you have failed to appreciate it. This is why we say that unless you are absolutely sure try the prescriptions in the parts that follow anyway. They act as a safeguard against making any false readings.

...............................................................

## KEEPING YOUR AIMS FLEXIBLE

Aims tend to divide down into short-term aims and long-term aims.

For the sake of simplicity, we can think of short-term aims as the aims you would like to achieve in the next twelve months. Because they are concerned with your immediate job situation, they are usually a little easier to define. They could include, for example, skills you want to acquire or experience you want to gain. They may link to your career grand plan or they may simply be a response to some need that has arisen in the day-to-day course of your work.

CASE STUDY: LES

'We have just received an edict from head office about reducing inventory levels. There are a number of new purchasing and stock control techniques on the market which I am not up to date with. Sometime in the next six months I need to get myself on a suitable course.'

Long-term aims are a little harder to deal with. Some people, like Greg, set themselves targets on what they plan to achieve within defined periods. Others are less sure about the direction they want to go in or, like Jackie, they are young people who feel they would benefit from more experience before they make too many decisions.

There are two extremes of conduct to consider here. The first is drifting about aimlessly with no clear ideas on where you are going and ending up achieving little as a result. The second is being too narrow and rigid in your ambitions and finding you fail to pick up on the best opportunities. Another case study will help us here, a true story, sad to say.

## CASE STUDY: JENNIE

Jennie worked in the group marketing department of a large company where she had been for the last six years. The work was mainly project based and, because of the company's diverse activities, it was varied and interesting. The shock for Jennie was considerable when a new group chief executive arrived and announced that the marketing department was to close and, with effect from a date in three months' time, companies in the group would be responsible for doing their own marketing.

Jennie was one of the few members of staff of the marketing department to be offered alternative work. This was the post of assistant to the divisional manager of one of the companies in the group – a small, fast-growing subsidiary involved in the design, manufacture and installation of specialist security systems. Jennie had put together a marketing strategy for this company recently and the divisional manager was very impressed with her work. The job (which was on the same pay and conditions as her old job) included the newly devolved marketing responsibilities but, as the divisional manager explained, the size of the business meant that this would not be enough to fill her time. She would also have to do some contracts administration and double up in the sales office when they were busy or short staffed.

Though Jennie liked the divisional manager and felt she could work with him, the more she thought over his offer, the more she felt it was not for her. Marketing was her chosen career and what she had done ever since she left university. Indeed her aim in life had always been to get a board level job in marketing – a job like that of her soon to be redundant boss – and she could see no way in which taking on a all-rounder role in a small business advanced her career in the direction she wanted it to go. She decided therefore to decline the offer and opted for redundancy instead.

Sadly for Jennie, finding a job in marketing comparable even with her old job proved decidedly difficult. After a period of unemployment she ended up doing a series of temporary assignments. Eighteen months later she is still looking for the right slot.

Jennie had never had the experience of being out of work before so it would be harsh to chastise her for failing to appreciate just how hard it can be getting back on the ladder once you've been pushed off. Yet what we can criticise her for is passing up the chance to widen her skills and experience and to open up her job prospects as a consequence. Even if the job in the security lighting subsidiary didn't work out, she would have lost nothing by giving it a try. And, who knows, she may have found the wider job brief more to her liking than she anticipated.

Like a lot of people (and without knowing it) Jennie has locked herself into the idea of a one-track career when the world doesn't accommodate that any more. Careers are no longer tidy and one directional: frequently they involve going sideways and even backwards to go forwards; frequently they involve taking the less than perfect option for the simple reason that the perfect option isn't there.

This ability to use what's available and to play it to your advantage is what marks out people who can operate successfully in today's world of careers. People who achieve what they want to achieve often do so by going along dog-leg routes. Being flexible and opportunistic is the key.

There is a further point in Jennie's case study: any opportunity to widen your skills and experience should be taken, irrespective of whether it fits into your grand career plan or not. There are no prizes today for narrowness. Indeed, with the ever increasing number of small companies and the fragmentation of many large companies into small autonomous business units, the demand is for people who can be all-rounders.

---

| GOLDEN RULE 2 |
| --- |

Master the art of the possible

---

..................................................................

# ARE YOU OVERREACHING?

Back to Greg on pages 22–3. You will remember Greg's aim of becoming a manager earning £30k a year was realisable as far as his company was concerned. There was nothing in his company's profile to suggest that they could not deliver what he wanted. The only item of doubt was Greg himself. Was he going to be ready for promotion into management within the two year timescale he had allowed himself, or was he simply being naive and over-optimistic? If the latter, because of his unrealistic expectations rather than any prob-lem with his company, he would be pursuing an aim that is not realisable and should therefore reconsider his goals.

Knowing when you are overreaching (trying to take a step too far or too fast) is not easy to determine. In a perfect world, Greg's directors would have a quiet word in his ear but, as we know, people are not always that frank. True, some companies have formal appraisal inter-views, but there is no guarantee that they will be conducted properly. But there is a bigger problem for people seeking the truth about themselves, which the following case study demonstrates.

CASE STUDY: ANDREW

Andrew, the manufacturing director of a large automotive components producer explains:

'For years I worked for this guy and I didn't know that he was putting me down. Being young and inexperienced I didn't see that block-ing off my promotion prospects was his way of exerting his authority over me and I took his

judgements on my job performance as gospel.
As I got older, however, I began to have doubts.
Finally I decided to put my belief in my own
abilities to the test and I went out and applied for
a few jobs. Four out of the five applications I
made turned out to be successful so I took the
best offer, said goodbye to my boss and my
career has never looked back since.'

What Andrew's story illustrates is that, at the
end of the day, any assessment of you in your
job is one person's view of another – in this
case the boss's view. It is entirely subjective
and that is the extent of its validity.

In Part 2 we will be dealing with communicating your aims: letting your company
(notably your boss) know exactly where you
are coming from and what your aspirations
are. The feedback from this kind of dialogue
will tell you a great deal about how your boss
views you and you will be able to form your
own judgements. If you sense the doors are
being shut in your face (for whatever reasons)
then this will suggest to you that, within the
context of your company, your aims are not
realisable. If you are a realist and a master of
the art of the possible, you will deduce that
you are flogging a dead horse and take stock.

## TAKING STEPS IF YOU SEE
## YOUR JOB IS UNDER THREAT

Once upon a time – and providing they kept
their copy books reasonably clean – people in
careers didn't have to concern themselves too

much about the security of their jobs. In the main, redundancy was something that happened to blue collar workers: a largely proletarian event. Those days, however, have long passed and no book of this kind would be complete without some mention of spotting when your job might be under threat.

You will remember that one aspect of profiling your company was to get you to assess its capacity to provide you with secure employment. We noted that this was not just a question of looking at its trading performance and spotting any potential decline in the demand for its products or services, but also of examining its culture and the personalities of people in decision-making roles. Of particular concern was the so-called 'hire and fire' organisation and, though few would own up to the label, there are many such companies about.

Losing your job can feel catastrophic. In many cases it is followed by a period of unemployment (with all the accompanying distress) after which you may end up taking the first job that comes along (often more distress). It can take a long time to get your career back on track.

Spotting when your job may be at risk is admittedly not easy, but there are some warning signs that you should never ignore:

- any kind of merger, acquisition or take over is usually followed by restructuring – meaning heads will roll
- a new broom arrives at the top (e.g. a new chief executive)
- the introduction of new methods or technology, tending to mean a need for fewer people.

Take particular note of these events if you

happen to have short service, since redundancy lists are often decided on the basis of 'last in, first out'.

What should you do in these circumstances? Get some options open for sure, and do it fast. For a start, get off as many job applications as you can and don't dilly-dally (see *Job Seeking* by Karen Holmes, also in the Career PowerTools series). Whatever you do, don't wait until you get your redundancy notice.

Redundancy is of course not the only reason why people's jobs come under threat. There are other circumstances where it pays to get some options open:

- you get a new boss: nine times out of ten it works out fine, but always be prepared for a clash of personalities
- you get warnings for some aspect of your conduct or performance. Be particularly concerned if you can't see any reason why you are being singled out
- you have the bad luck to be sick or you have family problems that cause you to lose time from work. Be warned that small companies and those that operate in fiercely competitive markets will have most trouble in coping with staff absence.

---

| **GOLDEN RULE 3** |

Spot the danger signs.

---

...........................................................................

# ARE YOU GIVING IT YOUR BEST SHOT?

A central message in this book is to treat your job as one of the best assets you've got. Look after it properly and it will look after you. What you put into it will determine what you get out.

From time to time we all have to ask ourselves whether we are giving our jobs the best shot we've got. Are we putting in all our skills, knowledge and effort or, for reasons best known to ourselves, are we holding back?

Sometimes people's aims are not realisable because they are not performing to the best of their ability. When they ask the question 'Why am I not achieving my aims?', the finger of blame points at no one except themselves. In extreme cases, not trying hard enough puts people's jobs at risk, and in the competitive world we live in today this is more likely to happen than it was in the past.

On the face of it, effort is something we can do something about, e.g. improve our performance by trying harder or going on courses to improve our skills. Frequently, however, people don't realise when they are not giving their jobs their best shot and, when they don't get what they want in life, they turn to grousing. As an example, listen to what Bob has got to say about his company.

CASE STUDY: BOB

'My pay here is a pittance. If you compare what I get with what people with my qualifications get in other companies you will see I am at least £5k down on the market. I've taken this up with the general manager time and time again, but all I get from him is evasive answers.'

But look at what Bob's general manager thinks about Bob.

## CASE STUDY: BOB

'Bob is one of those characters who has got it upstairs but he is off on the dot every night and never volunteers for extra work. The biggest problem with him is he is always grousing about his money. My attitude is, why should I pay him more when there are far more deserving cases in the office – people who may not be as bright as he is but who will pull out the stops when we need them to and who stay late when there's a backlog.'

Could we criticise Bob's boss for not being more up front with him? Let's put this to him:

'You'll never change Bob so I don't see the point. Besides, he's not a problem to me. His work is reasonable and I can put up with his grousing.'

None of us are particularly good at seeing fault in ourselves and it's far easier for us if someone else can point out where we are going wrong. Yet we can't bank on this happening. Your boss could be like Bob's boss and for reasons of indolence, apathy or simply not wishing to be drawn into painful conversations he or she may not be telling you if some aspect of your performance is not up to the mark. Part 2 ('Communicating your Aims') will encourage you to request feedback from your boss but, again, you can't rely on this being entirely forthright. As a failsafe, then, check when you feel a grouse coming on about not achieving what you think you ought to be achieving. Ask yourself if it could be your fault.

At this juncture, note the fine line between not trying hard enough and reaching beyond your capability (the condition we've described already). The symptoms are exactly the same – not achieving what you want to achieve – but the treatment is different. In the case of overreaching you stop what you are doing and take stock; in the case of not trying hard enough, you take note and step up your effort or seek ways of sharpening your skills.

### CASE STUDY: RONNI

'I work in sales as a major account executive. I went through a difficult period in my private life about two years ago and I know I made the mistake of letting it affect my job. I ended up with a warning to pull my finger out which – though I didn't like it at the time – probably did more than anything else to make me straighten my head out. The problem for me now, however, is that I think that this lapse in my performance is being held against me.

'A promotion came up recently and I reckon I was by far the best candidate – both in terms of my experience and ability. The bloke who got the job is a comparative newcomer to the company and there are glaring gaps in his product knowledge.

'Frankly, I am beginning to wonder exactly how long it is going to take me to redeem myself in the company's eyes. Five years? Ten years? Or, is there going to be a permanent black mark against my name? In which case, because I am ambitious, is it best for me to find another job?'

It is a sad fact of life that corporate memories can be very long when it comes to past errors and omissions. With promotions to top jobs, particularly, there is always the inclination for companies to want to 'play it safe' simply because too much is at stake. So, yes, effort to get your performance back on track frequently does not seem to get the reward it deserves. This is an aspect of what we will be referring to later in the book as 'the lifelong interview'.

Of course, Ronni may not be reading her situation correctly, but she is right to be suspicious – and right too to take her passing over for promotion as an amber light that the company might still be harbouring dark thoughts about her. What should she do? A try at the outside job market might be the best bet if she is looking for promotion in the short term. Any more amber lights should certainly put the matter beyond doubt (e.g. a poor pay review). Flogging on in a company where there are deep-seated misgivings about you is pointless.

........................................................................

# DEFINING YOUR AIMS

You should by now have:

- profiled your company and established whether it has the capacity to deliver what you are seeking to achieve
- examined where you may be overreaching (trying to go too far, too fast) – again within the context of your company
- made sure your aims are not too rigid and narrow; that you are honed to take

advantage of any good opportunities that
come along
- taken steps to cancel out any lack of
effort on your part
- considered whether any lack of progress
may be due to some past transgression
(where the company has put a question
mark by your name).

With this bit of fault finding completed, you
are now ready to move forward and look at
your aims. What should you be looking for
from your company? What items should you
be putting on your agenda? This, if you like, is
going to be your shopping list.


## Promotion

Taking on board the warnings we have given
you about narrowness, rigidity and the conse-
quent dangers of trying to pursue one-track
careers, it does pay to have some ideas on the
directions you want your career to go in,
otherwise you end up drifting round aimlessly.

### Thinking about promotion

- There is no harm in setting yourself
targets (see the case study of Greg,
earlier), i.e. that you want to be at a
certain level in your company within a
defined period of time. What you must
avoid, though, is allowing your targets to
get in the way of your flexibility and
opportunism. For instance, if Greg's
company happened to come along with
the offer of some opportunity outside
design and project management, he must

evaluate the offer for what it is worth.
The fact that it is there, sitting on the
plate, is a great selling point, but what he
must not do is turn the offer down
simply on the basis that it is not in
accordance with the target he has set
himself. Remember what we said about
successful careers these days often taking
the dog-leg route.

- Given the need for flexibility (and within
  reason), the more ideas you have the
  better.

- Don't rule out career changes. Increasingly
  these days, working lives take in more
  than one career (we are onto our third!)
  Be ready if advances in technology or
  market forces diminish the need for
  people with your skills. Be ready for the
  day to dawn when you feel like doing
  something else for a change.

- Break your promotion aspirations down
  into long term and short term. It could
  be that you have no promotion
  aspirations short term because, like Greg's
  colleague, Jackie, you may feel that your
  present job gives you all the scope you
  need to gather the experience and skills
  that are relevant to you at this stage. If
  you have no promotion aspirations long
  term (providing you're not like Joe and
  nearing retiring age) ask yourself seriously
  whether you are stagnating (see page 47)
  – stagnating is dangerous.

- Don't be afraid to dream. A little
  fantasising about the future does no
  harm. Certainly don't cancel anything out

because it seems too ambitious. Some
of the best success stories started with
a dream.

## Money

Most of us have views on what we ought to be
paid. A surprising number of us feel we are not
being paid enough. Treat money with caution
– particularly any opinions you have that you
are underpaid. What is a fair rate for the job is
highly subjective and the notion of a 'going
rate in the market' has practically disappeared
(a spin-off from the fragmentation of so many
of the large firms that once dictated pay levels
within areas and occupations and the arrival
in their place of small companies who negotiate salaries with individuals on a 'one-to-one'
basis). While we are very keen to see you get
the best deal that you can financially speaking, be careful that you don't fall into the trap
of:

- going over the top: asking for a big rise
  and finding all you achieve is putting
  your company's back up
- putting a label on yourself as being the
  kind of person who is always bleating
  about money.

Money is a subject that should be seen very
much in the context of your company. Form
an honest view of what they will pay. If they
are notoriously tight-fisted, then you are wasting your time putting in demands for a big pay
rise (back to the art of the possible again).
There is more on negotiating a better deal for
yourself in Part 2.

## Perks

Under perks come items such as your inclusion in the share option scheme or the company's private medical plan. Inevitably the subject of company cars comes up under this heading (too frequently, perhaps). With perks the context of your company is all important once again. Remember Terri-Ann on page 25? Terri-Ann wanted a bigger company car but her company had a fixed policy on the types of cars allocated to different grades of staff. Her ambition was not realisable.

## Job terms

You might want to negotiate (or re-negotiate) some item in your job terms.

CASE STUDY: JAY

'Last year I was asked to share responsibility for training with a colleague. This hasn't worked out and it has become a cause of conflict. I want all the job, not half of it, and if I can't have it, then someone else can do it.'

## Training

You want your company to keep your skills up to date and to provide you with training in any new skills you may need to do your job. Some training needs you diagnose for yourself, however, may not relate to your current job and you will have to decide what to do about these.

CASE STUDY: EVA

'I am keen to get French and German language skills. Currently I work for a small company which only deals in the UK market. For this reason I can't see them letting me have time off to go on a course.'

In these circumstances an alternative to asking your company to provide you with the training is to organise it yourself. In Eva's case, French and German language training is commonly available in the form of evening classes and, with the increasing availability of open access learning (including the Internet), practically any subject under the sun can be tackled in your own time.

## Experience

Experience enables us to do our jobs more fluently and proficiently. When situations arise we deal with them using our experience of how we dealt with them the last time they arose. We incorporate any lessons we learn into our experience (notably mistakes we made which we won't be making again). We gain experience from exposure to work situations and we learn from the example of those who are more experienced than ourselves. We expect our companies to provide us with opportunities to acquire experience. If these opportunities are not being made available then we need to say so.

CASE STUDY: CLARE

'I remember my first year in industry vividly. I spent most of the time sitting in an office on my boss if I could sit in on some of his meetings his retort was that this was not possible because his meetings were confidential.'

## Other aims

People develop all sorts of aims in the course of their work (potentially the list is almost endless).

CASE STUDY: RAJIV

'My company has been through difficult times and over the last three years the staff of my department has dwindled by natural wastage from six to two (a trainee and me). Now things are picking up and I find I am having to work six and sometimes seven days a week to keep on top of the work. The company is still operating a freeze on recruitment but I can't carry on working sixty hours a week. I need to negotiate a special dispensation to recruit an experienced member of staff.'

## STRUCTURING AND PRIORITISING AIMS

You may now have a long list of aims. It could be far too long to be of any practical use. What you need to do next is go through your list and strike out any aims that are:

- not realisable in the context of your company, i.e. you will be running your list alongside your corporate profile
- going a step too far

- trivial and unimportant
- realisable by alternative means (e.g. our example of acquiring language skills by going to an evening class).

Now prioritise. Do this by simply putting 1, 2, 3 etc. at the side of each aim. As a guide to doing this, rank your aims not just on the basis of how important they are to you but also on how quickly you want to achieve them. For this reason your short-term aims should be appearing at the top of your list. There are two points to this exercise:

- bowling in to see your boss with a long shopping list will do no good at all. If it is likely to induce anything, it will be panic
- you will do far better if you pursue one aim at a time. Not only will your mind be better focused but you will make a better job of focusing your boss's mind too.

You are now ready to move on to communicating your aims – the subject we will be dealing with in Part 2. Before that though, we'll look in a bit more depth at stagnation.

---

| **GOLDEN RULE 4** |

Manage your own career.

---

..................................................................

# STAGNATION: KNOWING WHEN YOU ARE IN A RUT

This is important. A lot of people are stagnating without knowing it. Stagnating is not just squandering away your life: stagnating is also perilous. People who are stagnating:

- under-achieve: they are standing still when they could be moving forwards
- lose their confidence
- don't keep their skills up to date – as a result their skills become obsolete
- become narrow: they start to see only one way of doing things
- become resistant to change
- turn into grousers.

If any of these labels fit you, then beware.

How do people start to stagnate? The case study of Tina gives some suggestions.

CASE STUDY: TINA

'I have been with my company doing the same job for the last fifteen years. During this time I have seen the company successively "delayered", meaning that the path along which I once saw my career developing has been gradually taken away.

'I hung on, waiting for better times to return, which they never did. In fact recently, with the appointment of a new managing director who has some very negative ideas on people and their careers, things have taken a decided turn for the worse.

'Because of these developments I made my mind up recently to try my chances on the outside job market. I applied for a position I saw advertised, attended two interviews and – to my amazement – within three weeks I had an offer of employment in my hand! But then, much to my surprise, I started to get cold feet. The reality of leaving hit me (having to say goodbye to colleagues and old friends). I began to have doubts, too, about whether I could do the job that was being offered to me. What first seemed like challenges started to appear as threats. I procrastinated. I asked for more time to think the offer over then, when the company started to push me for an answer, I took what I saw as the safe route and turned it down.

'In hindsight I think I made a mistake. What worries me more than anything is that I will never ever manage to pluck up the courage to leave.'

Poor Tina, irrespective of whether the new job was right for her or not, she is certainly suffering a crisis in confidence (one of the symptoms of stagnating we described earlier). Tina got herself into the rut she is in through no fault of her own but because her company changed from being a nice orderly place with clearly marked out career paths into a flat organisation. In short, the promotions she wanted became unrealisable and her experience proved it.

Reasons for stagnating usually encompass some or all of the following:

- flogging on in a company where your ambitions are not realisable (failing to profile your company properly and ensure that what it can deliver pairs with what you are looking for)

- overreaching: pursuing ambitions that are

beyond your capability and not taking stock when you find you repeatedly get passed by

- failing to put time limits on how long you are prepared to give your company to come up with what you are looking for (as Tina found, the years do slip by!)

- not giving your company your best shot (not putting in enough effort)

- flogging on in companies where you have blotted your copy book and where your past mistakes are being held against you

- having ambitions that are too narrow or rigid; finding you are waiting for years for the 'perfect' opportunity to come up; finding, sometimes, you're waiting for ever

- having ambitions that are too small (too easily realisable) – worse still, having no ambitions at all

- not managing your own career (leaving it to others to decide your future when the others in question may not be inclined or competent)

- as Tina did, waiting too long for the good old days to come back; indeed waiting for any kind of change that is not within your control.

You will see that this list draws together most of the lessons in this part. It demonstrates that stagnating is the result of not following a structured and disciplined approach to managing your own career.

An important footnote here: careers don't

stand still and it is wrong to describe stagnating as standing still. What is really happening is that slowly but surely you are slipping backwards. You are under-achieving, losing confidence, losing skills and all the other symptoms of stagnating that we mentioned. You emerge from a period of stagnation in a worse state than you went into it and it pays to remember this.

Because it is so hard to spot when you are stagnating and because stagnating has such dire consequences, here is a little tip. As a failsafe device put yourself on the outside job market at least once every five years (more frequently if you are in any doubt). This has a number of benefits:

- it will keep you in touch with the world and show you what other companies can provide

- it will tell you if you are overreaching (you won't get the jobs you apply for)

- it will give you an idea of the range of salaries available to people with your skills and experience

- it will keep you in touch with what the job market wants. It will alert you if your skills need an update or if the market is looking for skills you haven't got

- it will keep you in practice if for any reason you need to go on the outside market 'for real', e.g. if your job comes under threat

- by seeing the way other companies do things, it will help you to spot any narrowness in your own perceptions

- who knows, you may even be offered a good job!

What about Tina? Is there anything she can do about her situation? Tina's case underlines the point we made earlier – that you come out of a period of stagnation in a worse condition than when you went in. Tina's first task therefore, is to get her confidence back and she should be able to draw some strength from the fact she got offered another job so quickly. At least one company soon spotted she had some potential.

Should she go back on the outside job market? We would say no – at least not right away. For a start, she could be wrong about her company and she should set about doing a proper profiling exercise (it is never too late to do this). If as a result she does come to the conclusion that her ambitions are not realisable and if she can see no alternatives, then the outside job market may be the right place to be. This time, however, she has got to be serious about it and here is another reason why we think it would be better to pause before throwing herself back into job applications. She can use the break to re-examine her commitment to changing jobs and to steel herself up for saying yes the next time she's on the receiving end of a good offer. One thing is for sure: if she finds she gets cold feet a second time round it will have a very bad effect on her confidence.

Finally we would say to Tina, that if she does stick with her company she should heed all we have to say in the parts that follow about communicating aims and following them through. The references to flat companies in Part 5 should also make interesting reading to her.

......................................................................

# QUESTIONS AND ANSWERS

## No need to manage my own career

**Q** I see no need to manage my own career because my company (like Laura's in your example on page 14) makes a very good job of doing it for me. Can I take it therefore that your Golden Rule 4 doesn't apply to me?

**A** No, you can't opt out of managing your own career – not in today's climate. If you need any persuading on this, some of the worst cases of stagnation we have come across are people who have spent years in large paternalistic companies like yours. They suddenly wake up to the fact that the company has made all the decisions for them and they have gone in directions they never really wanted to go in. Take our advice: always have your own agenda (separate from the company's). Remember, too, that nice companies can change – sometimes dramatically and almost overnight.

## Corporate profiling: company taking away perks

**Q** Following a take-over, my company is slowly scaling down senior staff fringe benefits to bring them into line with our new parent company. First to go was our six weeks' annual leave (reduced to five), next came our retirement age (put up from 62 to 65) and now we hear that our company cars are going to be downsized. Naturally, no one is very happy but, from a profiling point of view, how should we be viewing these developments?

**A** If the reason for the changes is to bring you in line with a parent company then, as an aim, getting your perks reinstated would not seem to have a great deal of mileage. Whether you should view the whittling away of your perks as a reason for quitting your job is another matter, and the reality here is that you might be hard pushed to find another company offering a similar range of perks to the ones you enjoyed under the old regime. Also be very careful not to let your move on to the outside job market with all the accompanying risks be driven by a grouse (you need stronger reasons).

## Exposing black marks against your name

**Q** In Ronni's case (page 38) would it not be sensible for her to tackle her bosses and ask them (i) if the warning she had two years ago influenced their decision not to offer her promotion and, if so (ii) how long they propose to go on holding it against her?

THRIVE IN YOUR COMPANY

**A** In theory, yes, but in reality we suspect that her bosses might take the easy route and offer 'other reasons' for her non-selection. As to putting a time limit on how long the black mark stands, it is easy to say 'another twelve months' then find when the next promotion opportunity comes up in two years' time the same memories and misgivings are still there. With top jobs in companies, irrespective of what's been said before, there will always be the inclination to want to 'play it safe'. In our experience these stigmas can stick round for many years and it would be naive on anyone's part to feel that, at a point in time, the slate is magically wiped clean.

## Stagnating: too old to do anything about it

**Q** I am fully aware that I am stagnating, but I am on the wrong side of 45 so, in real terms, what can I do about it?

**A** In a way your need to avoid skills obsolescence, resistant attitude to change and narrowness is greater than it would be for a younger person. For example, if you had the bad luck to lose your job, these are precisely the kind of bad points a prospective employer would be looking out for in an over 45-year-old. Aims, having them and realising them, are not the preserve of any particular age group, though the nature of your aims will be different at different stages in your working life. If we take the example of skills updating, there is nothing to stop a 50-year-old seeking to do this. Is it realisable in your company? If so, go for it. If not, find other ways of updating your skills (e.g. go to an evening class). Most importantly here, don't start writing yourself off because you have reached a certain age.

## TICK YOUR PROGRESS

✓ Have aims that are realisable in the context of your company.

✓ Don't pursue aims that are not realisable.

✓ Realise your aims internally if you can (view moving on to the outside job market as your action of last resort).

✓ Have aims that are flexible.

✓ Master the art of the possible.

✓ Look out for when you may be overreaching.

✓ See the signs when your job is at risk.

✓ Give your job your best shot (never expect something for nothing).

✓ Face up to it when the company has got the down on you because of something you did in the past (where no amount of effort on your part is going to put matters right).

✓ Define and prioritise your aims so that you can tackle them one at a time.

✓ Accept responsibility for managing your own career.

✓ Don't allow yourself to stagnate. If you feel you're in a rut do something about it.

## Part two

# COMMUNICATING YOUR AIMS

**T**aking on board all you want to achieve, what is the best way of presenting your aims to your company? How do you make sure they get the message? In this part we will be looking at:

- the importance of making yourself understood: how messages that aren't clearly stated get ignored or misread

- distinguishing between stating your aims and grousing – making sure that you don't end up achieving little except putting up people's backs

- how appearing as a threat can be counter-productive; how companies go on the defensive when they feel their arms are being twisted

- using internal networking to further your aims

- timing your communicating right; using formal occasions such as appraisal interviews

- listening to feedback: using advice and criticism to move your ideas forward

- having stratagems you can go on using: making sure your messages are not just 'one shots' that you can never use again

- the importance of credibility; not doing anything that could cause the company to stop believing in you.

..........................................................................

# MAKING YOUR AIMS KNOWN

It's not uncommon to find the middle ranks in a lot of larger companies populated by bright, (in the main) younger people who feel that their promotion chances are being blocked. They see good jobs (jobs they would like to do) being offered to outsiders and they conclude, that:

*either* the company doesn't have a good opinion of them,

*or* the company doesn't promote its own staff.

In both cases, this is usually the signal to people that, if they want to get on, they are going to have to get out. Let's take an example:

## CASE STUDY: LIZ

Liz works for a chain of DIY superstores. She is in her early thirties, well qualified and keen to be promoted to a store manager's job, yet, as far as her company is concerned, she has given up hope. Recently she has seen three store managers' jobs filled by external candidates. At no point was she asked if she would be interested in the position.

Was it that Liz's company didn't rate her highly enough to consider her suitable for any of these posts, or was it a case of preferring outsiders?

CASE STUDY: LIZ

We asked the superstores' human resources director why the company didn't follow the path of internal promotion. Her response was:

'That's simple. There's no one in house who would be interested in taking on store management responsibilities. If there was, believe me, we would be more than happy to give them a try.'

But what about Liz?

'Liz? You surprise me. Firstly she has never said that she wants promotion. Secondly, these vacancies came up in other parts of the country and I would never have put Liz down as being interested in relocation.'

So who's at fault here? The human resources director for:

- taking Liz's silence to mean contentment with her present lot and no greater ambitions
- assuming without checking that Liz would not be prepared to relocate?

Or was it Liz who was to blame for not articulating her aims properly?

Sadly, there are a lot of people like Liz: people who have been passed by out of ignorance or because their aims have been misread. This illustrates one of the great truisms about life skills – that communicating is the hardest thing of all to get right.

Even in companies where relationships are close, the assumption is often there that the other party is the one who should be 'saying something'.

---

| GOLDEN RULE 5 |
|---|

Take responsibility for communicating your
aims.

---

..............................................................

# COMMUNICATING ISN'T GROUSING

The fact that so much misunderstanding can
(and does) creep into communicating career
aims begs the question why this should happen? Why do we feel awkward about broach-
ing the subject of what we want from our
companies? What causes us to stay silent or, in
some cases, to feed out false signals?

Happily we live in a less deferential world
than previous generations so fear of the boss
and what the boss might do if we speak out no
longer preys on the minds of most of us.
Rather, the problem is that we like to sound
positive when we talk about our jobs, and least
of all we want to sound like grousers. No one
loves a grouser. We all know a grouser or two
and we don't seek to emulate them. Saying
we're not being promoted as fast as we would
like to be or not being paid the salary we
expect to be paid comes closer to grousing
than most of us can feel comfortable with –
and this is why the words tend to stick in our
mouths. We are much happier when we can
talk about the good things in our jobs, the
things we enjoy and the things we are pleased
the company provides.

Communicating aims isn't grousing and,

from the start it is important to make firm distinctions between the two in your mind.

---

| **GOLDEN RULE 6** |

Never grouse.

---

## How to avoid grousing

- Steer clear of accusations and accusatory language, e.g. 'Last year you said you would do something about my salary but you never did.' Apart from being a trade characteristic of grousers, accusations carry the double-edged liability of being threatening. People on the receiving end of threats rarely react in the way you expect them to. In the case of companies it tends to throw them on to the defensive (see pages 65–7) – meaning you don't get what you want.

- When talking about your company keep in the first person plural ('we' and 'us'). For example: 'We said last year we would look at salaries ...' sounds much better than 'You said last year you would look at salaries ...' The impression that it is you versus the company is taken away.

- Don't bring up your aims during the course of everyday conversations about your work. Keep discussion to meetings that are specifically for the purpose (meetings that you prepare for).

- Avoid the urge to repeat yourself (another grousers' trade mark). Keep any statement of your aims simple and in any discussion say it once only.

- Avoid sneers and cynical remarks when something is being explained to you. Even if you don't like what you are hearing, listen and record the facts. Best of all, make no comment at all until you have had the chance to reflect.

- Don't harp on history. Even if the company treated you shabbily at some point in the past, don't bring it up unless it has a direct bearing on your current aims. Usually past history surfaces solely to score points. All it really proves to the person listening is that you are walking round with a chip on your shoulder.

- Put your remarks in the context of 'I like my job, I like the company, I want to make my career here and this is the way I would like to see my career develop ...'

- Use questions in place of bald statements, particularly questions that are designed to elicit the other person's opinion, e.g. 'How do you feel I would benefit from a course in finance for non-financial managers?' has no grousing overtones, while 'I've been given no training in how to understand accounts' has. This is a particularly useful tactic where the point at issue is subjective – as with pay. For example, contrast 'How do you feel my pay lines up with my responsibilities?' with 'I'm underpaid and it's time something was done about it.'

- Don't state a problem without offering a solution. Grousers like to whinge and whine but rarely point the way forward. You can often dispel any impression of grousing by outlining the outcome you want, e.g. promotion to the board within the next three years. Note: this is also compatible with good managing of your career.

- Don't make statements that don't have an aim, e.g. 'People who work in trading divisions get performance-related pay, but in head office we don't.' If you are trying to get a pay rise, address yourself to that aim. What people in trading divisions get is irrelevant because you don't work in one and sounding off about them comes across as straightforward grousing. What's more, the recipient of this information might miss the point you are really trying to make.

- Don't preface any statement you make with a negative, e.g. 'My career isn't moving very fast and I want to talk about my prospects for promotion.' The first part of the sentence adds nothing and carries the risk of subsequent discussion being about whether your assertion is correct or not.

........................................................................

# COMMUNICATING AIMS WITHOUT MAKING THREATS

When communicating your aims to your company, it is hard to resist telling them what you would do if your aims are not met – the most frequently uttered words being along the lines of 'I would have to look for another job'. The reason why you do this, of course, is to fire a warning shot across their bows. You're serious about what you are saying and you don't want the boss to think he can get away with his usual trick of nodding along with you then doing precisely nothing.

Warning shots can come in other forms too. For example, Darren has been working very long hours for nearly a year and he wants his company either to pay him for his overtime or recruit someone to assist him. If they don't, Darren tells them, he will make sure he's out of the door at five o'clock every night.

The trouble with threats – or anything that could be construed as a threat – is they rarely have the effect the deliverer intends. Attention switches straight away from the aim under discussion to how the company would respond if the threat was carried out. Sometimes the aim gets completely forgotten.

The difficulty for you when you start accompanying your aims with threats is that you are never quite sure of the end game. For example, your company may simply dig their heels in: 'We don't respond to threats. Please yourself whether you stay with us or not.' Equally they may have to say no to you for other reasons and this then puts you in a tricky position. Do you back down and lose credibility? Or do you carry out your threat and look for another job? You may not have been totally serious about leaving of course which means you will be moving out on to the job market without commitment. In Darren's case the outcome he wasn't expecting was a rap on the knuckles from his company and a reminder that his terms of employment required him to work extra hours when necessary.

If you should succeed in sending a shiver up your company's spine and the prospect of you packing your bags and leaving does have the intended effect of forcing their hands, then a fact you will have to face up to is that you can never pull the same trick again – at least with any conviction. It is an example of what we will be referring to on page 75 as a 'one-shot stratagem'. In the business of achieving aims, getting to where you want to get is frequently a question of persisting over long periods. Stratagems, therefore, need to be repeatable, so stratagems using threats are automatically ruled out.

---

| **GOLDEN RULE 7** |

Never make threats.

---

Threats, can be construed from other aspects of your behaviour that fall short of explicit words and you need to be aware of this. In particular be careful about:

- accusations
- raising your voice
- emotive language ('I have had to suffer ...' 'It isn't fair ...' etc.)
- threatening body language (wagging fingers, glaring looks, folded arms).

..............................................................

# PREPARING WHAT YOU WANT TO SAY

In Part 1 we looked at defining and prioritising your aims, and we advised you to attempt to resolve one aim at a time in the order of their importance. You now need to ask yourself a further question: how do you feel your selected aim is going to be received? Back to your corporate profiling here: since the receiver is going to be your boss and since your boss is someone you know well, you should be able to make a good job of this. The intention here is to put the spotlight on any aim that might cause raised eyebrows – in which case, consider whether there might be any benefit in breaking your aim down.

## CASE STUDY: SEVE

'I am looking to improve my salary by £7k a year and, with increased responsibilities I have taken on, I feel that this is more than justified. However, I know my boss and I know the shutters will come up as soon as I mention £7k. My aim therefore is to get a £4k increase now, then come back for the rest next year when hopefully my performance with my new responsibilities will add weight to my case.'

Fine, this is all part of asking yourself what is realisable and what isn't. In this instance, what is realisable at this point in time (the art of the possible).

Are there any snags? Only this: your boss might read your suggestion that a £4k hike in your salary is all you are looking for and feel that you have gone back on your word when you ask for another £3k next year. Our advice is to tell him the whole game plan (the two stages). Apart from anything else, if you are going to have a problem with realising your aim, the sooner you know about it the better.

Having decided the content of what you

want to say, the next stage in preparation is deciding how to put it over.

By now you will have taken on board the warnings we have given about grousing and the dangers of accompanying your statements with threats. We advised you to keep all your remarks positive and within the framework of 'I like the job, I like the company, I want to make my career here and this is the way I see my career developing.' The rest – the gist of your aim – you should plan to put across as follows:

- Keep it brief. Remember the more you say, the easier it is for misunderstandings to creep in. Don't repeat yourself.
- Resist the urge to 'dress it up'. Speak plainly. Avoid meandering explanations. The only issue here is ensuring that your message gets across clearly.
- Remember to use 'we' and 'us' when you talk about the company.

## HANDLING DISCUSSIONS ABOUT YOUR AIMS

You now know what you are going to say and how you are going to say it. The next step is to set up a meeting with your boss. Inevitably he/she is going to want to know what the meeting is about, so pre-empt the question by saying you want to talk about your career and requesting half an hour in private. Suggest after hours or a time when interruptions are least likely.

Of course, you may work in a company where an appraisal system is in place and where an appraisal interview is held every six or twelve months, giving you the perfect opportunity to enter into a dialogue about your career aims. Check, though, if you want to talk about your salary: some companies exclude salaries from the subjects they discuss at appraisal interviews and this may have to be done on a separate occasion, e.g. at your annual salary review.

The best way to handle the discussion with your boss will depend on:

- your boss's personality
- the magnitude of your aim. For example, if you are asking to go on a one day course, it would be reasonable to expect a quick yes or no answer
- whether your boss has the authority to agree to what you want.

As with all meetings you need to have an objective. The objective in this case is to state the aim you want to achieve and to get a reaction. Depending on how good you've been with your guesswork, the reaction may or may not be one that surprises you.

## Conducting the meeting

- Try to bring the meeting to a close as quickly as you can. Don't protract the discussion any longer than necessary – once you've said what you want to say and you've got the boss's reaction the meeting is over as far as you are concerned.

- Don't get locked into arguments. If the boss is hostile to your ideas leave it at that. You are a step nearer to establishing your aim is not realisable – though an exit line along the lines of 'Perhaps we both need to think things over' leaves the door open for your boss to have a change of heart. Remember to say thank you for listening.

- If your boss is non-committal and says 'I'll think about it' again, leave it at that. Questions like 'How long do you want to think about it?' are best left alone. 'I'll think about it' is often a coded message that the boss has to run your ideas across someone higher up the ladder.

- Your boss may actually tell you that the decision on what you want rests with higher authority. Find out here whether you will have to make the running yourself or whether your boss will take your case up for you. If the latter, get a measure of how sympathetic the boss is. Your aim here is to have your boss on your side.

- If your boss is in agreement with what you are saying, end the discussion on that happy note. Don't, as some experts would have you do, start pinning the boss down to time scales because it could set off alarm bells and undo the good work you have already done. We will be dealing with how to progress your aims in the next part. For now, just go home and, when you get there, give yourself a pat on the back because you have done what you set out to do.

- If the reaction is negative yet constructive, e.g. 'You're right to have these ambitions but you need more experience in x, y and z before you have any chance of realising them ...' listen to what's being said, refrain from too many comments then go away and reflect. It could be that your aims will benefit from incorporating the boss's ideas, i.e. the advice is good advice.

---

| GOLDEN RULE 8 |

Listen to advice and criticism.

---

..................................................................

# HOW DID YOU GET ON? EVALUATING YOUR PROGRESS

The object to what we have done so far is to ensure that your company, in the shape of this key figure (your boss), is aware of your aim and that you are not in the same position that Liz back on page 60 found herself in. In other words, you have moved forward and taken the first step towards achieving your aim.

CASE STUDY: GAENOR

'I don't see why this is necessary. My boss is perfectly aware that I want to make a move into marketing.'

Is she? Before you jump to any conclusions, ask yourself how she is supposed to have gleaned this information. A chance remark in conversation? Something you said at your interview when you applied for the job? Something she may have dismissed as being half serious? Something she may have forgotten? The point here is that these misunderstandings of people's career aims are so frequent and the cause of so many problems (why people leave companies unnecessarily and make risky job moves) it is worth being doubly sure. In short, if you are in any doubt about whether your message has been received, get knocking on the boss's door right away.

What was the boss's reaction to what you had to say and how should you read it?

## Agreement

Here the magnitude of what you're asking for comes into play. If, for example, you are asking to update your skills by going on a course (i.e. something fairly minimal), agreement is simply that. Presumably you move on to booking a place on the course and the aim is achieved. If, however, the point you're communicating is that you want to see yourself in a top management slot within the next two years, agreement has no immediate consequence. But what you have done here is to put a mark in the ground – something you can refer back to at points in the future. What you have done also is to programme your boss, e.g. if some good job opportunity comes up in the company and if your boss is asked if anyone in the team would be interested, your name has a much better chance of popping into the frame. Best of all, however, is the tacit little warning you have delivered: you are ambitious, you want to get on and if the progress you want to make isn't forthcoming you are going to get itchy feet – in short, the company runs the risk of losing you. You have made the point that you are not going to be content to become part of the woodwork – and you have got this across without entering into the risky business of making threats.

## Rejection

If you run into a brick wall – a straightforward 'no', 'never' or 'no way' – is this telling you that your aim is not realisable? Perhaps, but keep your mind open to two possibilities:

- this is the boss's view and no one else's, i.e. your boss's boss might have a completely different opinion (more on this in Part 3)
- your boss may be having a bad day. If so, by leaving the door open as we suggested, you are giving your boss the chance to backtrack.

Rejection seems a completely negative event and it may be hard to see the progress you have made. The progress, in this case, is progress towards establishing that your aim is not realisable. But don't, whatever you do, let rejection and the reasons given for it, become the cause of an argument. Listen to what you're told and disengage (leave it at that). For instance, arguing with your boss as to whether his or her assessment of you is fair will achieve nothing.

## Somewhere in between

Knowing your boss's character will tell you how to view any equivocating. If you are getting a lot of possibles and maybes, this could be because your boss always equivocates. Prick your ears up though for any good points of advice and criticism – the kind of points that you could incorporate into your career aims. Finally, let matters rest there. You have achieved what you wanted to achieve. The boss knows where you are coming from and, in the case of bigger long-term ambitions, the little tacit warning has been delivered that you are not the kind of person who is going to feel happy about being passed over and, if you are, it could be the reason for you deciding to take your talents elsewhere.

Keep notes of these discussions (the date when it took place and a précis of what was said and agreed). There is more on notes in Part 3.

..............................................................................

# AVOIDING THE 'ONE-SHOT STRATAGEM': COMMUNICATING IN WAYS THAT YOU CAN GO ON USING

Making your company aware of your career aims fully and formally is a major step forward and you should not underestimate the value of what you have just done. You now have a framework in place for moving the dialogue forward and for the dialogue to become the basis of your future relationship with the company. However – and here is a big warning – you will not be able to do this if you have used a 'one-shot stratagem'.

Threats are a good example of one-shot stratagems. You tell the company you want a big pay rise and if you don't get it you'll go out and find another job. Fine, the company is sufficiently terrified by the prospect of you leaving and taking your skills elsewhere, they cave in. But the problem for you is when you come back in twelve months' time and try the same approach again. This time, the company will smell a rat and, more to the point for you, a tangible slice will be taken off your credibility. Will they be so quick to give in this time? What's more, how will they view you generally? A serial blackmailer? Certainly not the kind of person anyone would want in the senior management team.

There are other examples of one-shot stratagems. Here's one:

### CASE STUDY: CHRIS

'I wanted a pay rise of around £5k, mainly because I wanted to get my daughter into private education. Instead of asking for £5k, however, I put in for £10k and let them beat me down.'

This person's problem would be if he tried to use the same approach again. A slice would go off his credibility.

---

**GOLDEN RULE 9**

Stay credible.

---

......................................................................

# HOW TO PUT IN FOR A PAY INCREASE

As we noted when we looked at corporate profiling, pay is a highly subjective and emotive business and, because of this we have chosen to give it some additional coverage. After all, what is a fair day's pay? Is it to do with some vague notion of a market rate, or is it how we view ourselves in the performance of our jobs? Whichever it is, how do we establish the comparators and when we have got them how do we go about putting them to use?

Pay is such a complex issue it is best to start by going back to basics. Why is it people feel moved to ask for more pay? What brings the issue on to the agenda in the first place? It may be because:

- you feel you are not being paid the 'going rate', i.e. your company lags behind the market. Your evidence for this may often be anecdotal, from reading job ads in newspapers, or from colleagues who have left

- the quality and quantity of your effort is not recognised. Comparators are probably other people in the organisation who are less proficient or who work less hard

- your differentials are not equitable, e.g. Mark: 'My boss gets paid £20k a year more than I do, yet I do the lion's share of his work'; e.g. Alice: 'My staff get paid commission. In good months they can be earning more than I do, but guess who is left to deal with all the aggro!'

- you need more money to finance some aspect of your personal life. House purchase or moves up the housing market are a frequent stimulus for people to ask for rises.

To earn more money and to be better off in material terms is a perfectly respectable ambition. Yet fundamental to all questions of more pay is your company's ability to deliver. In fact it all goes back to your profiling again – in asking for more money and from what you know of your company, is your aim realisable? Does your bid for more pay stand any chance of coming off?

'Ability to deliver' is a difficult quality to determine and several factors may need to be taken into account. For example:

- your company's culture – is it a good payer or is it a bad payer? Does it have a tradition of being tight-fisted when it comes to handing out rises?

- trading performance – a highly profitable company will obviously be able to do more on the pay front than one that is losing money

- differentials – is giving you what you want going to give the company problems in other quarters? With the rise you are seeking, how will your salary compare with that of your peers and your boss?

- salary structures – does your company have formal salary scales, e.g. a range of salaries for a particular level of staff? If so, will the rise you are after put you through the ceiling of the scale? What flexibility is there for allowing this to happen?

The really big problem for you is that you may not have much of this information to hand. Salaries are a secretive subject (in some companies, highly secretive). For example, do you know what your peers are paid? Do you know if there are salary bands that apply to you and, if so, what the maximum is?

The other and possibly more important half of the equation is how your company views you. They may make all sorts of flattering remarks to you at your appraisal interviews, they may be constantly giving you pats on the back for doing your job well, but will this prevent them turning ashen faced when you walk in and ask for a £5k rise?

## Tips on asking for a pay rise

- Don't be driven by envy and don't be kidded into thinking everyone's doing better than you are. Stick with your own agenda. The only items that matter are your value to your company and your company's ability to deliver.

- To assess your company's 'ability to deliver' go through the factors we listed in Part 1 (as far as your knowledge allows). If there are any strong signals to suggest you are heading into a brick wall (such as your company has just announced record losses) back off immediately. If not, proceed to the next bullet point.

- Ask yourself seriously whether you are going over the top (the penalty is loss of credibility). Try putting yourself in your company's shoes. What justifies what you are asking for? Have your job responsibilities increased? Have you done something exceptional recently?

- If you feel you are being paid less than the going rate for someone with your experience and qualifications, put it to the test. Two easy ways of doing this are:
  - try applying for a few jobs and see what the companies concerned are offering
  - talk to some employment agencies: ask them what kind of salary someone with your experience and qualifications could expect to get on the outside market.

- Your company probably has an annual salary review. Obviously a bad time for putting in for a rise would be after the review has taken place.

- Remember the advice about not prefacing your remarks with a complaint ('I am underpaid', 'The work I do here is unrecognised', etc.). As an opener, try a question designed to elicit your boss's opinion, e.g. 'How do you think my salary reflects someone with my skills and experience?'

- Don't get into a barter. If you think another £2k on your salary is justified then say so and stick to it. You will gain all-important credibility from this.

- Don't be inflexible. If your company comes up with another way of increasing your salary (e.g. in stages or by way of a performance-related bonus) then listen to what they have to say.

- Don't get into arguments about salary. If your company is not prepared to pay you what you want, then leave it at that.

- Keep your ears open for advice and criticism. There could be a good reason why your company is holding back on your pay – in which case you need to know what it is.

There is more on negotiating pay in Part 4 (see page 139).

......................................................................

## QUESTIONS AND ANSWERS

### Too useful

**Q** The reason I don't get promoted is because I am too useful to the company in the job I am doing. How do I deal with this?

**A** Be careful that this is not just your interpretation and don't, whatever you do, let your feelings become the subject of a grouse. The way forward? Do as we suggest and make sure first of all that your company is aware of your ambitions. If you are right (if you are being held back because you are too useful) your company will quickly realise from your remarks that you won't put up with this treatment for much longer and that they run the risk of losing you if they can't offer you the promotion you want. If you are wrong (if there are other reasons for your lack of progress) then hopefully you will pick up some clues from the feedback.

## Good jobs are always filled by headhunters

**Q** With my company there have been a number of instances where good job opportunities have been farmed out to headhunters, so ambitious people like me don't get a look in. In most cases, the first we hear about these opportunities is when someone starts (someone who has been headhunted from outside). What can I and other people in my company do about this?

**A** Retaining the services of a headhunter (or executive search consultant) is very costly and no right-thinking company would go down this route if someone was available internally who could slot into the vacant job. Yes, there are instances where an employer could be seeking someone with external experience for a specific reason (e.g. experience with a successful competitor), but if your company is repeatedly going to headhunters it tends to mean one of two things:

*either* they have scanned the internal talent and found that it falls short of their needs

*or* they have assumed (like Liz's human resources director) that for one reason or another, the internal talent would not be interested.

What can you do? Flag up your ambitions along the lines we have suggested in this part and progress them in the way we will be suggesting in Part 3. Really, what you have got to do is to get your message over to your company *before* they bring in the headhunters. By being methodical and proactive in this way you will soon learn whether your company views you as 'not suitable' for these opportunities (and why) or whether they are passing you by because they are unaware of your ambitions. From this point you can proceed accordingly.

## Communicating your aims in writing

**Q** Surely the best points are made by putting them in writing. In my case, I have a CV in which I have listed my various career aims. Would I not make a better job of communicating these aims by simply handing a copy to my boss?

**A** The main function of a good CV is to get you interviews and, it goes without saying, that one of the advantages of pursuing career aims internally is that the door is normally open to you. What is slightly worrying about your suggestion is that you might be trying to avoid a face-to-face discussion with your boss (because you feel uncomfortable about it). Whether the idea appeals to you or not, face-to-face is the best way of ensuring there are no misunderstandings and picking up any nuances from the feedback. By all means give your boss a copy of your CV, but do this after you have had your discussion.

TICK YOUR PROGRESS

✓ Make sure you have communicated your aims.

✓ Take responsibility on to yourself for getting your message across.

✓ Don't confuse communicating with grousing.

✓ Don't make threats.

✓ Keep your credibility intact. Don't blow it by trying to work fast ones on your company.

✓ Listen to advice and criticism. Use feedback to fine-tune your career aims.

## Part three

# GETTING THE
# DEAL YOU WANT

**H**aving communicated your aims, the next step is realising them. In this part we will be looking at:

- the importance of putting over the right image and giving every day your best shot

- adding to your value to the company and boosting your bargaining power

- your visibility on the corporate scene: keeping your face in the frame

- giving to your company: investing your talents with a good payback in view

- auditing your progress: spotting where your message may not be getting across and taking corrective steps

- using internal networks to advance your aims

- evaluating opportunities: when to say yes and when to say no to offers made to you; putting the art of the possible into practice

- negotiating techniques and what part they play.

## ATTACHING IMPORTANCE TO EVERY DAY

Contrast what your company knows about you with what an employer would learn about an outside applicant in the space of, say, two job interviews. If you're smart enough you can pull the wool over an interviewer's eyes in a couple of 60–90 minute sessions, but you won't be able to do the same with people who have known you day in, day out for a number of years. Idle Jack who puts in for an internal promotion based on his record of hard work will soon be laughed out of the door.

There is another side to this coin, however, and it is this: people who are well thought of in their companies automatically qualify for getting what they want. If Beavering Bill wants to climb the ladder, the chances are his company will be there to give him a helping hand. Most of all, Beavering Bill's company won't want to see him leave.

These are all aspects of what we call the lifelong interview: the process of continuous assessment to which we are all subjected in the day-to-day performance of our jobs. We have seen one example of the lifelong interview already: the case of Ronni on page 38 and how a lapse from grace at some point in her past was held against her for several years. The lifelong interview can work in your favour or it can work against you, but what you must never be in any doubt about is its power.

---

**GOLDEN RULE 10**

Give your best to every day.

---

..............................................................

# ADDING VALUE TO YOURSELF

Your ability to get the right deal for yourself ultimately rests on two factors:

- your company's ability to deliver the deal (the essence of the material in Part 1)
- your value to the company (how they view you in relation to the deal you are seeking – whether in their eyes you are worth it).

Giving your best to every day will enhance your value to your company. Your case will have far more clout to it than that of someone who has been less diligent on the lifelong interview front. Not only will the company feel reluctant about acceding to the demands of someone whose efforts have been half-hearted and/or inconsistent, but they will have few concerns if that someone decides to seek his or her fortune elsewhere.

There are other ways in which you can add value to yourself:

- **By adding to your skills base**

  *Gareth:* 'I can now program every machine in the machine shop. I am the only person in the company who can do this.'

- **By adding to your experience**

  *Samantha:* 'As part of a cost-cutting exercise, the company closed the human resources department and responsibility for human resources management was heaped on my shoulders.'

- **By adding to your qualifications**

  *Kelly:* 'I am a civil engineering graduate working for a large construction company. The company sponsored me to do an MBA by studying part-time at the local university.'

All three of these people have added value to themselves: Gareth because his range of skills is unique; Samantha because she is successfully combining the HR function with her own, thereby saving her company money; Kelly because with her MBA she will be better placed to take on bigger responsibilities.

In all three cases – and for different reasons – the employers of these people would be sad to see them go, meaning two things:

- they will be keen to keep them happy by giving them what they want
- though nothing is certain in this world, they are less likely to find their names on redundancy lists.

With this business of adding value to yourself, what will not have escaped your notice is that Gareth, Samantha and Kelly have also enhanced their attractiveness to other employers, so as far as their companies are concerned, the stakes are raised. Adding value therefore equates to increasing bargaining power. The bargaining in this case is done with unspoken words because both sides know exactly what the score is. If your company can't provide you with what you want, they know full well that there will always be someone else to oblige.

Samantha's case illustrates three very interesting points, which are highlighted in her story, below.

## CASE STUDY: SAMANTHA

Samantha explains how she came to take on the company's HR function.

'The instruction to shut human resources came in the usual form of edicts from Head Office: a terse three-line memo from the chief executive to our divisional director – strong on deadline dates and completely lacking in any suggestions as to how we were supposed to assimilate the work of HR once the manager and his team had been made redundant. We fired back a few protests of course, but predictably these fell on deaf ears. Pretty soon we realised that this was about headcount. Two of the trading divisions had run up enormous losses in the last twelve months and the chief executive wanted to see significant savings in payroll costs.

'Faced with a no choice situation we settled for spreading HR's functions round the management team (for example, each manager was given responsibility for doing his or her own recruiting) but this still left a core of jobs that would suffer from dispersion. It was at this point that the divisional director suggested that I should take on these jobs, though frankly I felt I had more than enough on my plate already. Was there the chance of more pay? Not with the current clamp-down on costs, the divisional director explained, though he promised to do what he could as soon as the opportunity arose.

'Don't ask me whether I'm being taken for a mug. I prefer to think that I will benefit from the widening of my experience and that some day somehow my willingness to take on extra tasks will work in my favour.'

The three interesting points are:

- the benefits of adding value are not always obvious
- the opportunity to add to your value can arise from situations that, on the face of it, look 'bad', e.g. being asked to do more work for no more pay
- in the down-sized, de-layered, fragmented, headcount-slashing world we live in, there are lots of opportunities like this.

A further point is that the opportunity to add value by broadening skills and experience is readily available in small companies (small businesses and small autonomous businesses that make up the constituent parts of larger groups – companies like Mike's on page 15). Here willing pairs of hands can often build up extensive portfolios of responsibilities. The magic words are 'leave it to me.' (There is more on this in Part 5.)

---

| GOLDEN RULE 11 |

Take every chance to add value to yourself.

---

........................................................................

# VISIBILITY

Keeping a high enough profile on the corporate scene is important because the good job you are doing for the company needs to be seen. Every organisation has its unsung heroes but, unfortunately for them, they are not the ones who receive the medals. As in real war, to get recognition the brave deeds need to be performed in front of the officers and the simple point here is that any success you have (e.g. any praise for the company won by your efforts) needs to be transmitted upwards. Sometimes the transmitting upwards will be done for you – in which case, so much the better. Sometimes, however, you will need to take responsibility for doing the transmitting yourself. Immodest? That really depends on the way you put it across. That the company has won praise is a simple fact. Your involvement is another fact. The juxtaposition of the two facts should be sufficient for someone to make the necessary connections.

Visibility is not, however, just for the glory moments. To work for you properly it has to be part of your everyday plan so, unless you happen to be in a particularly high-profile job, you will need to give some thought to how you are going to keep your face permanently in the corporate frame.

How do you do this? The key here is to be the positive team player at all times: the one who comes up with solutions when there are problems; the one who volunteers for extra work when the heat is on; the one who always has a useful contribution to make. The spotlight automatically falls on you, but there is a further point here and an important one: the visibility you have created is associated with the right things, e.g. willingness, good ideas, putting the company first – in other words, things that add to your value and increase your silent bargaining power. Conversely, if visibility associates you with the wrong things (being late for work, not completing tasks to deadlines) it will subtract from your value.

---

| **GOLDEN RULE 12** |

Make yourself visible.

---

Another (important) way of ensuring visibility is by asking for guidance and advice.

..............................................................

# 'GIVING' TO YOUR COMPANY

With any investment, what you put in largely determines what you get out. The same goes for your job. It will pay you back what you give to it. Conversely, if you give it nothing, it will give you nothing in return.

The brick walls a lot of people run into when they try to advance their careers are indirectly of their own making. The brick walls are there because their companies see them as people who don't contribute and, if we refer back to the case of Bob the Grouser on page 37, we see an example. The reason Bob's boss declined to put up his salary was because he was off on the dot every night and never volunteered for extra work. If we tried putting it to Bob that he would enhance his chances of getting the rise he wanted by being a bit more 'giving', his reaction would probably be to want to see the money first. If we told him to forget the money he would probably view the suggestion with indignation or mistrust. Short of ditching his attitudes, there is not a lot of hope for Bob.

By giving to your company freely and without restriction you are opening the door to their largesse (if they have any). Put another way, you are removing one more barrier to getting the deal you want.

---
| GOLDEN RULE 13 |

Don't hold back with giving your time and effort.

---

..........................................................................

# AUDITING YOUR PROGRESS

To sum up, you should now have reached the point where you have:

- established that your aims are realisable within the context of your company (as far as you can tell)
- communicated your aims to your boss and listened to the feedback
- picked out good points in the feedback and incorporated them into your aims
- got the agreement from your boss that your aims are realisable (the shutters haven't come up).

What you need to do next is review your progress periodically to see if you have moved any closer to achieving your aims and, if not, why not.

We suggest you carry out these review procedures systematically and to a timetable. If you are subject to appraisals then a good time to have a review of your progress is just before your appraisal interview. Being systematic is important. It ensures that:

- your career aims don't slip on to the back burner (because you are busy in other directions)
- you don't let up on your boss (allow him or her to procrastinate)
- you don't cop out of your responsibility to manage your own career
- you have a safety net in place to prevent you drifting into stagnation.

In your review the first item on the agenda is to remind yourself of the timescale you put on achieving your aim. Was it a short-term aim or a long-term aim? Review your progress under these headings:

**Short-term aims.** When you carry out your review it stands a good chance (by definition) that the aim has been achieved. You have been on the course you wanted to go on; you have had your four-week secondment to the legal department – so, great, you can put a tick by the aim and move on to the next one (remember what we said about tackling your aims one at a time).

**Long-term aims.** These are harder. For example, if the aim was to be offered a partnership within five years, then there probably won't be much to show in the way of progress when you do your first review. Here one of the chief objects to reviewing is to check for bad signs. Bad signs are warnings that something is going wrong.

**Bad signs.** The classic bad sign when you are looking for promotion is to see someone being brought in from outside to do the kind of job that you would like to do. This time the company (your boss) knows about your ambitions so it can't be a misunderstanding – you really have been passed by! There are other kinds of bad sign too: Here are two examples:

CASE STUDY: DAWN

*Dawn:* 'I agreed with the MD that my salary needed to be increased by £4k to take account of my new responsibilities. Imagine my shock when I received notification of my January salary review and found that I had only been awarded the standard increase.'

CASE STUDY: JAMES

'I joined this company because it gave me the chance to work overseas and I have pushed for an overseas posting at every opportunity. The company has now decided to close its overseas offices and appoint a network of local agents instead.'

## DEALING WITH BAD SIGNS

A bad sign is usually the signal to get on your bike. In Dawn's case, the company has reneged on the deal (she can't trust them any more). In James's case, the goal posts have shifted (his aim is no longer realisable).

Sometimes, however, the bad sign is not what it seems, as can be seen from the case study of Nick.

CASE STUDY: NICK

Nick is an area sales manager working for a large pharmaceuticals company. At head office, the company has its own management development centre – part of which is a sales training facility.

For the last year Nick has had his eyes on becoming a sales trainer and he made a point of mentioning this ambition to his boss, the regional director, at his last appraisal interview. Nick is now facing a situation where a new sales trainer has been appointed from outside the company – and to add insult to injury it is someone who previously worked for a competitor.

Nick explains:

'I asked to see my boss straight away and I guess he knew what was coming because he had some of his answers ready. The top and bottom of it was that, because he has no involvement in the appointment of management development centre staff, my boss had about as much idea as me as to what was going on. What struck me as lacking, though, was that he had not thought to communicate my interest in sales training through to the head of the management development centre. If he had, then presumably I would have been given a chance to apply for the job. When I mentioned this to my boss all he could say was that he was sorry.'

Was this a communications boob, or should the company have had better arrangements for advertising vacancies internally?

There is a third alternative, of course – that Nick as a good manager of his own career should have spotted the potential difficulty and taken steps to prevent it. For example, was there anything to stop him transmitting his sales training ambition direct to the head of the management development centre, the person in whose remit this lay?

Nick: 'You must be joking. What you are suggesting is going behind my boss's back. I can tell
you that wouldn't please him in the slightest.'

First point first – bad signs are not always what
they appear to be. If you see a bad sign the best
way to proceed is as follows:

- Speak to your boss immediately. Don't
  delay, because this could create the
  impression that you are not over-
  concerned.

- Remind him/her of your previous
  discussions. Explain your concern.
  Encourage him/her to put himself/herself
  in your shoes.

- Listen to the explanations.

- If, as in Nick's case, the explanation is a
  communications failure, seek agreement
  on how to avoid repetitions. With Nick
  the agreement should be about who is
  going to speak to the head of the
  management development centre. Nick
  should be seeking to do this himself, but
  if his boss insists on being the conduit,
  Nick needs to keep check that the
  conversation has taken place.

After you have had this discussion with your
boss go away and reflect on the explanations.
If for any reason you are not satisfied with
them (e.g. you feel you are not being told the
truth) then revert to reading the bad sign as an
indicator that your career aims are not realisable and take stock from there. If finding
another job seems to be the only answer then
don't delay in getting yourself out on the

market. Letting these situations fester is rarely good. In any event, if there are any more bad signs, read this as a very positive signal to start getting off job applications.

....................................................................

# WHAT TO DO IF NOTHING HAPPENS

A common outcome is where your communicating of career aims is followed by silence. You have had a pleasant discussion with your boss but then the subject of your ambitions is never mentioned again, hence when you come to review your progress you find your progress is nil. At what point do you read into these silences that something has gone amiss? Even if no bad signs have manifested themselves when does it become time to hit the alarm bell?

Silences have a number of possible explanations:

- the aim was a long-term aim so there is nothing sinister about the fact that there has been no progress

- the boss has forgotten. In the downsized modern world we live in where there are fewer pairs of hands at all levels and where the pace of work has been accelerated by information technology and advances in communications, there is greater and greater scope for genuine oversight

- the boss doesn't have the authority (this may not be apparent)

- the boss has had second (negative) thoughts and doesn't like to tell you

- the boss has been higher up the ladder and been given a no. The delay is because he/she is putting off telling you

- unknown to you the company's circumstances have changed or are about to change, e.g. the company is up for sale meaning promotions, salaries and larger items of expenditure have been put on ice.

This list goes on, but what is important with anything you do now is that you begin to form an opinion on whether your career aims are still on track.

Here we have no better advice than putting your head back in the lion's den. Find out from your boss what's going on and listen carefully to the feedback. An appraisal interview forms a natural occasion for having this kind of dialogue but, if your company doesn't have appraisal interviews, do the time-tabling yourself: a chat about your career aims at least once every year is advisable.

Warning: don't do as some people do and automatically assume that no news is bad news. No news is no news. Keep an open mind. Don't throw yourself on the outside job market just on the strength of 'hearing nothing.'

## CASE STUDY: LESTER

Lester is a Chartered Accountant in his late thirties. He is the financial controller of a large printing company and he has been in his job for the last five years. His predecessor held a seat on the board and Lester sees no reason why he too should not be given a directorship. He has made this point to the managing director at his last two appraisal interviews and, each time, the managing director has agreed with him in principle but then come up with plausible reasons why it can't be done at the moment. On both occasions the interviews have ended on a note of 'let's wait and see'. What Lester can't decide is whether he is being strung along or not – and if he is, the reason for it. His big concern, though, is that he could be waiting years for his directorship and still be disappointed. What he wants to avoid at all costs is reaching the age of 45 and finding he is no further forward. If he needs to change jobs to realise his ambition to get a seat on the board of a company, then he would prefer to do it sooner rather than later.

Lester is right to have these concerns. Countless people find themselves hanging on for years for promotions that never materialise and this illustrates one of the biggest difficulties with long-term career aims; how long do you give your company to come up with the goodies? The penalty for getting this wrong is that you end up stagnating. You end up squandering away the best years of your life and the consequences for you are very serious indeed. Your best years don't come round a second time.

The answer here is to take charge of the situation (all part of managing your own career). What's a reasonable period of time for your company to come up with what you are looking for? One year? Two years? Plum for a figure then say to yourself: 'This is how long I am going to give them', and stick to it. If the company doesn't deliver in that period, form the view that your aim isn't realisable. In other words, included under the heading of aims that are not realisable should be the aims that are only realisable in open-ended or over inordinately long periods of time. Don't be messed about with this – remember, it's your career that's at stake.

......................................................................

# RECORDING YOUR PROGRESS

Make notes every time you carry out a review of your progress. Record your thoughts (including the dark ones) and summarise any points for action. Tell yourself what progress you are expecting to make by the time your next review comes round. This recording is important for a number of reasons.

## The importance of record keeping

- With the passage of time it can be difficult to recall precise details. A lot of water can go under the bridge in a year and, the busier you are in your day-to-day job, the easier it is for your memory to play tricks. Notes made at the time can be a valuable aid when it comes to picking up the threads again and this is especially important with long-term aims where you will be reviewing progress over a number of years.

- Aims can start to drift and, each time you do a review, it pays to remind yourself where you started out with them. This is best done by referring to your notes. A typical example is the person who started with big ambitions but whose ambitions became diluted by what they saw as 'reality'. The usual explanation here is that the ambition wasn't realisable in the first place, i.e. the company is wrong, not the ambition. The inclination, however, is to tone the ambition down to make it fit the corporate profile. Beware, letting your career drift in this way is a common cause of under-achievement and the best way of ensuring you don't do it is by being methodical about recording how your career aims have developed.

• It is a check on you that you are using good feedback. Take Sharon as an example:

**CASE STUDY: SHARON**

Sharon worked in credit management and she was keen to get into sales. Sharon, however, had never learned to drive and her boss, the company accountant, made the suggestion some time ago that this was something she ought to do (a career in sales might be difficult otherwise). But to this day Sharon has done nothing about booking a course of lessons for herself. As far as the company accountant is concerned, therefore, she has ignored his advice – so what is his reaction going to be if Sharon continues to press for a transfer to sales? How much support is he going to give her? Sharon, of course, never intended to alienate her boss. She hasn't done anything about learning to drive for the simple reason she hasn't got round to it. Yet a note in Sharon's progress log would have acted as a sharp reminder to her that she had omitted to act on her boss's good

good advice and the repercussions would hopefully have dawned.

- It adds a sense of importance to what you
  are doing. It gives proper weight to the
  business of achieving career aims.

Warning: keep your notes at home. Don't
leave them in the office where your boss or
your colleagues might come across them.

..........................................................................

## DEVELOPING AND USING INTERNAL NETWORKS

Networking, using your contacts to advance
your career can be divided down into:

- getting to know the right people
- making the contacts work for you.

Striking the right acquaintances clearly links
in with your visibility, except this time we are
talking about visibility beyond your immediate circle – and herein lie some dangers.

Never be in any doubt that networking is a
powerful career tool and, consistent with the
analogy, it can do a great job for you if you use
it properly but, if you don't, it can deal you a
lethal blow. Like all powerful tools, networking needs careful handling. (See *Powerful Networking* by John Lockett, also in the Career
PowerTools series.)

To illustrate one of the difficulties, think
about Nick again (see page 97). Nick, you will
remember, missed out on a chance to make
the move into sales training he had set his

heart on because his boss had not thought to convey his ambition to the head of the company's management development centre (the person responsible for appointing sales trainers). We asked Nick why he hadn't taken matters into his own hands and made contact with the head of the management development centre himself. Nick's reply was that his boss would have been put out if he felt that Nick had gone behind his back.

Anyone who has worked in management knows that ignoring these sensitivities is something you do at your peril. So in Nick's case, he was right to be concerned. Not only did he spot the need to keep his boss on his side, he also realised the potential for the boss to put a spoke in his wheel. Here are two examples from our case book:

## CASE STUDY: ERROL

Errol fixed up a transfer for himself from one part of a large decentralised group to another. His boss was furious about being presented with a *fait accompli* and refused to release Errol for twelve months – far too long for Errol's new job to be kept open for him. In the end the group chief executive had to be called in to arbitrate. His displeasure at having to do so was made very apparent to all concerned.

## CASE STUDY: CAROLINE

Caroline applied for an internal promotion without her boss's knowledge and got turned down. To this day, she suspects that when her boss was contacted for a reference she suffered the fate of being damned by faint praise.

---

| **GOLDEN RULE 14** |
| --- |

Keep the boss on your side.

---

Networking across corporate boundaries needs handling with special care. In particular, networking done with the express purpose of advancing your career (as it would have been in Nick's case) needs always to be done with the full knowledge and consent of whoever you report to.

But with all this emphasis on going through your boss and keeping your boss on your side, the question arises as to what to do if for any reason you feel that your boss is the fly in the ointment? If he/she is the one standing in your way what can you do about it?

Going over your boss's head is clearly a high risk game and something you only do with your eyes wide open. Even if you win the day, the chances are the relationship between the two of you will never be the same again.

Frequently, however, going to the boss's boss doesn't have the outcome you hoped for. You find the same line is taken and this reflects:

- the boss and the boss's boss share the same opinion, *or*
- the boss's boss feels it is incumbent on him/her to support the boss (irrespective of the merits of the case you are putting forward), *or*
- the real fly in the ointment is the boss's boss and the boss has simply been acting as his/her mouthpiece.

Our verdict on going over the boss's head is that it should be seen as an action of last resort, perhaps the final thing you do before putting yourself on the outside job market. If you really feel the boss has got it in for you there is probably not a lot of hope for the future anyway.

Making the right acquaintances outside your immediate orbit tends to have few problems in integrated companies with strong central cores because the infrastructure for networking is in place (e.g. social functions, company management meetings, etc.). The same goes for smaller companies where your face will be known to everyone pretty soon after starting. This emphasises an important point about internal networks: in a lot of cases they don't require special cultivating; they are the natural outcome of your day-to-day work.

Where, however, networking presents a special challenge to people is in the growing number of decentralised, loosely strung together and geographically scattered companies. Here, there is often no infrastructure for developing networks – or it is minimal – and extending your circle of contacts calls for proactive measures and a bit of resourcefulness. You will find advice for people working in fragmented companies in Part 5.

Step two to networking is making your contacts perform for you. This is the most important part and here we go back to the link between networking and visibility. Visibility, you will recall, is only good for you when it associates you with the right kind of things. For example, if your visibility associates you with being late for meetings or forgetting to attend, then plainly it won't do a lot for you. This, in turn, relates back to your lifelong interview and the importance you need to attach to consistency and giving your best every day.

To see how these various lessons come togther in practice, look at the case study of Rachel.

## CASE STUDY: RACHEL

Rachel has been put in charge of a new division – a business providing specialist advice and consultancy in the field of health and safety. One of Rachel's first tasks is to appoint an operations director who will effectively be her number two. For this job she needs someone with a lot of hands-on experience in doing risk assessments but, before advertising the position or talking to executive search consultants, she has been casting her mind round possible internal candidates. One face that has come into the frame is Patrick. Patrick is currently working as a maintenance manager in one of the group's commercial divisions and he is keen to get promotion.

Rachel knows Patrick because, for a number of years, they have represented the company on an industry working party. Patrick is very knowledgeable in risk assessments, but an aspect of Patrick that troubles Rachel is the fact that he is always complaining about his boss. Doubtless some of these complaints are justified, but the last thing Rachel wants is a number two whose loyalty she can't be sure about. Too much is at stake for Rachel – the new division, the opportunity she has been given to prove herself in a top management job – hence she decides reluctantly to give Patrick a miss.

She picks up the phone and puts in a call to an executive search consultant who has been recommended to her, reflecting as she does that it was a pity from Patrick's point of view that he could not have been more careful about what he was saying to her.

Sadly for Patrick he botched his lifelong interview and the network relationship he struck
up with the upwardly mobile Rachel did him
no good at all. What he thought was a
harmless bit of belly-aching turned out to be
the dose of poison he slipped into his own
chalice.

So what lessons can we learn from Patrick?

- You are not always aware when you are
  networking.
- Today's peers can be people who have a
  great influence on your career in years to
  come.
- How important your lifelong interview is
  – don't ever show yourself in anything
  less than your best possible light.
- How recollections stick.

In summary: view networks as a natural outcome of your day-to-day work. Focus any
effort on making networks work for you and
do this by paying constant attention to your
lifelong interview.

..............................................................................

## NEGOTIATING TECHNIQUES

Look at the case of Ruth.

CASE STUDY: RUTH

Ruth is a high-flying sales executive working in
the contract catering industry. This year alone
Ruth has brought in business totalling 20% of
the company's annual gross turnover enabling
the board to embark on an ambitious expansion
plan. The problem for Ruth is she is paid what is
largely a straight salary; there is an incentive

element but it is subject to a ceiling. Ruth feels her efforts need better recognition and she puts this to her boss, the sales manager, suggesting two alternatives:

*either* a one-off lump sum bonus
*or* a removal of the ceiling on her incentive earnings.

The sales manager was in broad agreement with taking away the ceiling but said he would have to fly the idea past the managing director. Two weeks later, however, he came back with a 'no'. The MD wanted to keep a cap on sales incentive earnings, he explained to Ruth, mainly to ensure that differentials with other key members of staff were maintained (people who didn't have incentive plans).

Predictably, Ruth was not very pleased with this answer and, as soon as she got back to the office, she phoned up the chairman of her company's biggest competitor. Finding her reputation for getting business had preceded her, she spent the next few days being given the red carpet treatment: an invitation to have lunch with the competitor's directors then, by the end of the week, a job offer from them with a good basic salary plus open-ended sales commission giving Ruth the potential to increase her earnings by about 40%.

Back at the office she showed the offer to her boss who was clearly shocked at the pace of events. Would she stay if the company could match the figures she had been offered? Ruth said she would think about it and her boss went off to see the MD. As a result, Ruth got the package she was looking for and she turned down the offer from the competitor on the basis she would be better sticking with the devil she knows. On the whole she feels pretty pleased with her exercise of bargaining power. The MD has been a bit frosty with her lately but Ruth figures he will get over having his arm twisted.

We have all known a few Ruths: people who get what they want by putting their notice in (or threatening to). So what mileage is there for the rest of us in imitating the technique? Why can't we all achieve our aims by being bought off?

A few observations first:

- Ruth is in a high profile sales job. She is very visible as far as her MD is concerned. This worked greatly to her advantage.

- Ruth has pretty powerful bargaining clout. She has added to her value enormously by performing effectively in her job.

- Trade competitors who sense a killing for themselves by importing knowledge and contacts can usually put enough icing on the cake to make their job offers attractive.

- There is no guarantee with the competitor that Ruth will go on being successful. For instance, if their pricing is off kilter no amount of wonderful salescraft will get signatures on contracts.

- After the red carpet treatment, the competitor will feel more than a bit miffed about being turned down. Soon it will get back to them that Ruth has been bought off and they will suspect that this was her game all along, i.e. that Ruth was using them to blackmail her company. They won't be quite so welcoming to Ruth next time she comes along. In fact,

Ruth shouldn't be too surprised to find the door slammed in her face.

The subject we are looking at here is what part negotiating techniques can play in getting the deal you want. In Ruth's case the negotiating technique she has employed is the blunt-edged weapon. Yes, if your stock in the company is high (if your visibility is good and if you have plenty of bargaining power) it stands a good chance of coming off, but there are risks and it pays to know what they are:

- Ruth is getting icy stares from her managing director. Naturally he is not pleased about what has happened but, as Ruth points out, he will probably get over it. What he won't do, however, is forget and, though it may not rate as a black mark on Ruth's character, it will certainly be a point of recollection if, for example, she is ever being considered for promotion. Is someone who goes out and gets another job whenever decisions don't suit them the kind of person the company wants in its top management team?

- Ruth's company isn't really comfortable about paying her so much money and this is a problem with arm-twisted deals. She is an anomaly – she is already giving the company differentials headaches and in future she will be viewed in a totally different light. What happens, for example, if her performance levels out? How supportive is her company going to be?

- Is it a one-shot strategy? What happens next time she wants to negotiate a deal with her company? If she goes on confronting her company with offers from other employers, isn't there a point when they are going to say enough is enough?

- In Ruth's case, what happens next time there is a salary review? Won't she be viewed as overpaid? Won't there be a tendency to give her less than the going rate of increases just to bring her back into line?

- What would happen to Ruth if her company dug their heels in and refused to be blackmailed? Presumably she would have to accept the competitor's offer – either that or lose credibility.

- If she does accept the offer, won't the competitor also view her as being highly paid? What happens if she doesn't perform to their liking? What happens once they have milked her of her knowledge and contacts?

The message here is that arm-twisting your company with job offers from other employers is a high-risk game and you should not play it if:

- you can't afford to take risks. If your personal and domestic circumstances are such that you can't take the downsides
- you are not 100% confident about your bargaining power
- you are not prepared to go through with leaving.

But given the risks, what are the alternatives

for Ruth? How else could she employ her
negotiating skills to get the deal she wants?

Her boss seems to be the crucial figure in all
of this:

- He is broadly on her side.
- He is the person talking to the MD and,
  in Ruth's company, the MD is the person
  holding the purse strings.
- He is most aware of her silent bargaining
  power (as sales manager, the potential loss
  of business if Ruth moves to a competitor
  will impact directly on him).

Given that the MD has given the thumbs
down to removing the ceiling on the incentive
scheme because it could encroach on differentials, could Ruth not go back to her other
alternative: the one-off lump sum payment?
Ok, so her boss didn't go for the idea the first
time but, given the MD's intransigence, perhaps it is something he could reconsider?
Short of that, does he have any other ideas on
how the company could deal with giving Ruth
the recognition she deserves? In other words
Ruth should keep going with her negotiation –
the slow drip, drip on the stone – and all the
time her silent bargaining power is driving the
message home. Finally she reaches the point
where she may have to conclude that the
company can't deliver and then she can take
stock properly (i.e. with all her options still
open and without putting herself in the stark
choice position of having to take a job with a
competitor or lose credibility).

With the modern job market there is plenty
of potential for bad moves, and a lot of people
have made bad moves because they have
played the high-risk game of trying to beat

their companies over the head with job offers from other employers.

Not put off? Happy to take the risks? OK, but before you do anything check your terms of employment. Ray's case study will illustrate why.

### CASE STUDY: RAY

'I work in a design and development role and because of the work I have done, my company now has a considerable technology lead in the market. My pay has been a sore point with me for some time and at a seminar I attended a month ago I bumped into the technical director of one of our biggest competitors. We got into conversation and one thing led to another then a few evenings later he rang me up and offered me a job heading their research and development section at a salary £10k in excess of what I earn. I asked him to put the offer into writing, which he did, and I then took it to my boss making the point that I would be accepting unless the company had something better to offer me. The response I got, however, was not the one I was expecting. My boss got out my file and showed me a copy of my terms of employment. There in black and white was a restraint clause forbidding me from joining any UK based competitor for two years. Talk about having egg on my face!'

Increasingly these days companies are seeking to protect themselves from any activities of former employees which will damage their businesses, notably:

- joining competitors
- using confidential information
- poaching staff.

There is a question at the end of this chapter about the enforceability of restraint clauses.

........................................................................

# EVALUATING OPPORTUNITIES

Success, getting the deal you want, is clearly a moment for elation. If it's a good deal (a significant move forward) it might even call for a celebration. But what you can congratulate yourself on most of all is that your approach has worked:

- You profiled your company and worked out what it could and could not deliver.
- You communicated your aims.
- You got the deal you wanted by persisting and completing.

---

**GOLDEN RULE 15**

Always complete.

---

A problem you may face, however, is arriving at the point where you are not sure whether you have completed or not. This happens where the company comes back to you with something different from what you proposed and here you have to decide what view to take. Should you say yes or should you say no? When should you be flexible and when should you stick with your original ideas and keep going?

In the second of our Golden Rules we introduced you to the art of the possible – two important aspects of which were:

- avoiding aims that are too rigid or narrow
- taking advantage of what's there.

There is a fine line between being flexible and accepting a deal you shouldn't be accepting because it will take you in directions you don't want to go in. Often it's hard to know which side of the fine line you are standing on.

## CASE STUDY: AZRA

For some time Azra has been pushing to get into a job where she can use her languages skills. Finally her persistence paid off and she has been offered a position in the company's overseas licensing department. The problem for Azra is that her move is not to be accompanied by a pay increase. She will stay on the same salary and be reviewed, as usual, at the end of the year. The work in the overseas licensing department carries much bigger responsibilities and Azra feels that this isn't fair.

What are the options for Azra?

*either* she can stay silent, take the job and learn to live with the fact she feels underpaid

*or* she can stick out for the right salary.

Both options of course carry risks. If she stays tight-lipped she runs the risk of feeling disgruntled. If she speaks out (says yes to the job and no to the money) she runs the risk of the job being offered to someone else.

A dilemma? Not really because, when you think about it, what Azra is trying to do is achieve two aims at once:

- getting the job she wants
- getting the company to deliver the right salary package.

Understandably therefore she is finding this difficult. Our advice to Azra? Take the job, give it your best shot, build up a bit of a good track record then start to work on the salary. Don't, whatever you do, poison your mind with thoughts that the company is trying to rip you off or short change you. Often these situations reflect nothing more than the company wanting to see you settled in your new job and starting to perform before they increase your pay.

## CASE STUDY: CLARKE

Clarke is a mechanical engineer who has been trying to get into his company's instrumentation department for some time. Yesterday his boss called him to his office and offered him a job working for a new division involved in the commissioning of capital equipment. The job is a good job but it isn't Clarke's pet subject (which is instrumentation) and he feels that by accepting the offer he will be kissing goodbye to his real ambition. After all, won't his company expect him to put down roots in the new division? Won't this automatically disqualify him if any opportunities in instrumentation happened to come up in the future?

Clarke's situation may be even trickier than he thinks. Saying no to the offer could send out a (wrong) signal that he is not the go-getter everyone thought he was and, as far as promotion is concerned, he could find himself being written off. Yet there is a genuine concern here: that if he takes the job in the new division his company won't be plying him with any further offers (at least not for a while). And if he seeks to avoid this fate by flagging up a continuing interest in instrumentation, it could convey the impression that his commitment to his new job is less than whole-hearted. So what should he do? What would you do if you found yourself in this situation?

The first question Clarke needs to put to himself is whether his getting into instrumentation aim is too narrow. For example, is it a case like Ed's (see page 24), where the department he has his sights on is small and where opportunities to get in are few and far between? Also it would be interesting to know why Clarke hasn't succeeded in achieving his aim previously. For instance, has he had any interesting feedback from the feelers he has put out and has he taken account of this feedback? Most importantly, does any of the feedback indicate that the company may not feel he is suitable for instrumentation and is he ignoring this because it isn't what he wants to hear? From honest answers to this bit of self-interrogation Clarke should be able to form a view of his chances of getting into instrumentation. The honesty part is important. We see many cases of people who have stuck out for hard-to-realise ambitions for years and years. The result, inevitably, is frustration and under-achieving.

Another question for Clarke is what's so magic about getting into instrumentation? Where did the idea come from in the first place and where will it lead him to once he's there? The point to asking himself these questions is because a lot of job ambitions on closer scrutiny turn out to be little more than the baggage people have been carrying round with them from distant points in their pasts. We can quote the case of Mary who has been harbouring an ambition to get into marketing for the last fifteen years. The reason? She did a business degree and found marketing the most interesting part of her course. The marketing department in her company consists of two clerical staff engaged in updating the company's price lists and sending out mailers, i.e. a classic career cul-de-sac. So what is Mary playing at? What she has clearly not done is let her ideas develop. Neither has she taken account of reality. In fact, she has allowed her ambitions to become rigid and now she is paying the price. The real opportunities in her company are in sales which is where she is working but, because of her rigid ideas she has allowed these opportunities to pass her by. The antidote to rigid ambitions? Spot them and dump them. Quickly.

Of course, Clarke's bit of self-inquisition may have exposed neither of the twin sins of narrowness and rigidity, meaning it could be right for him to stick with his original ambition. But, in turning the offer in the new division down, he has clearly got a big communications task on his hands:

- He must be very careful to explain his reasons ('I want to get into instrumentation. If I take the job in commissioning capital equipment I will be going in a direction I don't want to go in but I don't want the company to read my decision as lack of ambition ... [etc.]').

- Notwithstanding this, he must stand by for evidence that his communicating has failed. Despite his carefully chosen words, his company could still write him off as far as promotion is concerned.

- If so, he needs to get back in there and beef up his message.

- If the beefed message doesn't work, he will have to face up to the fact that in the company's eyes his image has changed. Visibility has gone against him and he is associated with the wrong thing (not interested in promotion). Sad though it seems, this could be the signal to him to try the outside job market. Either that or stagnate.

Modern careers tend to have no tidy pattern to them and people who succeed in today's downsized, fragmented and insecure world are people who don't lug baggage round from the past (old ideas that are no longer relevant) and who condition themselves into saying yes. Appreciate most of all that going forwards means going sideways and sometimes going in directions you have never previously considered. Occasionally, too, it means going backwards and you should be ready for this. At the end of the day, all that is important is you keep going. If you do, you will find the future opens up for you in diverse and often interesting ways.

...............................................................................

# QUESTIONS AND ANSWERS

## Adding value: cornering knowledge

**Q** Surely an obvious way to add to your value and increase your silent bargaining power is by keeping any knowledge you have gained strictly to yourself?

**A** True: if you are the only person on the grounds who can program the software on a machine and if the alternative to using you is calling in a programmer from the software producer at enormous expense, then you will have a lot of silent bargaining power. Most companies aren't stupid, though, and they are quick to spot situations where someone is hogging the knowledge and they respond by taking steps to put a stop to it. More importantly perhaps, what you are suggesting has the probability of being a one-shot stratagem. If you are pursuing an aim, attention will be focused on your silent bargaining power as intended ('Crikey, if he leaves we will have no one who can program the so and so machine …'). The alarm bells will go off, then someone else is trained up to program the software and this particular aspect of your silent bargaining power is taken away from you.

## Visibility difficulties

**Q** I work in export sales. I cover Scandinavia and I work from an apartment/office in Stockholm. My company is based in London and, apart from two sales meetings a year, my only contact with them is by fax or e-mail. How does someone in my position make themselves visible?

**A** People with remote reporting points do have a problem with visibility: 'Out of sight, out of mind' can soon turn into 'out of sight, completely forgotten'. Our advice is to view this as a challenge and put your mind to thinking out ways of heightening your profile.

For instance what about sending your boss a monthly report (something along the lines of a newsletter)? You know your boss so you know whether such an initiative would be welcome or not. The main point here is that having recognised the problem you need to take steps and do something about it.

## Are restraint clauses enforceable?

**Q** Not to put too fine a point on it, my silent bargaining power with my company rests largely on the damage I could do to them if I went to work for one of our competitors. I am subject to a restraint clause rather like the one in your example on page 116 (I can't work for any UK-based competitor for three years after leaving) yet I have always been under the impression that it would not be enforceable in a court of law. Is this true?

**A** The enforceability of restraint clauses is a subject all on its own. Broadly speaking, the wider a restraint, the less chance it has of being enforceable. For example a restraint preventing you from working for any competitor world-wide for a period of three years would have less chance of passing the legal tests than one where the restraint is confined to UK-based competitors and for a period of twelve months. This would be particularly the case if your company only traded in the UK. In your case the three years sound a bit steep, but a court of law would look at all the circumstances before deciding whether the restraint was reasonable or not. The point to mentioning restraint clauses, however, was not to invite you to start questioning their validity but to warn you that, if you are considering the high-risk strategy of using a job offer from a competitor to beat your company into submission, check your terms of employment first. Finding yourself faced with an injunction would not be a very desirable outcome for you, would it?

## TICK YOUR PROGRESS

✓ Attach importance to every day (your lifelong interview).

✓ Boost your silent bargaining power by taking every opportunity to add to your range of knowledge and skills.

✓ Be visible and make sure your visibility associates you with things that will count in your favour.

✓ Don't expect something for nothing: put in the effort before you look for the reward.

✓ Keep a check on your progress: don't let attention on achieving your career aims waver or lapse.

✓ Watch out for bad signs.

✓ Don't squander your best years away; put time limits on how long you are going to give your company to realise your aims.

✓ Keep notes on your progress (never rely on your memory).

✓ Keep your boss on your side.

✓ Don't play high-risk games unless you can take the downsides.

✓ Get the best results by being persistent.

✓ Complete and find out where you stand.

## Part four

# ASPIRING TO TOP JOBS

**F**or people who are ambitious, the prospect of moving into top jobs opens up sooner or later and this is where different rules apply. Among the topics we look at in this part are:

- what to do when the doors to top jobs don't open for you

- knowing your level of competence: when could you be exposing yourself to risk by taking a step too far?

- politics: steering a course through conflicting interest groups

- getting the right reward; what you can and can't achieve

- reducing risk: negotiating soft landings when things go wrong.

...........................................................................

## GLASS CEILINGS

You have done well up to now, you have climbed the ladder in your company success-fully but, just as you approach the top rung, you find for no apparent reason that your progress grinds to a standstill. You have been in the same middle-management job for a number of years but the door to the board-room remains stubbornly closed. Inevitably you start asking yourself 'Is this as far as I'm going to go?', and in bleaker moments you may even wonder if your face fits. It is then that the paranoia can really start.

'In my firm it's definitely a case of the old school tie.'

'All the partners are men. Because I'm a woman I don't stand a chance.'

'They've got something against me but I don't know what it is.'

It seems like your head is up against a glass ceiling: you can see what's on the other side but you can't get through to it.

Before you start jumping to too many wild conclusions about why your once glittering career seems to have ground into gridlock, run through the following checklist of reasons for people not making it into top jobs. See if any of them might apply to you.

## Reasons people don't get top jobs

- Taking out non-executive directors, it's not untypical these days to find the boards of even large companies made up of no more than two or three people. On closer inspection a lot of these companies are flat companies and should be viewed as such (see Part 5).

- Do you work in a small company? If so, directorships or partnerships usually involve ownership of equity and the existing directors or partners may not be happy to see equity dispersed any further. This is especially the case in companies where equity is in the hands of a family.

- How are your company's finances? If they

are trading at a loss or if cashflow is giving them problems they probably won't be in the mood for appointing any more senior people (even retirees and leavers won't get replaced).

- Is your company involved in a merger or take-over? Is it up for sale? In such circumstances, top management appointments are often put on hold (sometimes for quite long periods).

- Turning to you, is there any reason why there might be a black mark against your name. Remember the lifelong interview. With top jobs companies play safe.

In any of these situations, aspiring to a top job will fall into the range of 'difficult to impossible' on the realisable scale. The promotions you've had up to now have been OK but, because of the special circumstances surrounding top jobs, it is going to be hard for you to go any further.

What do you do now? Take stock, of course. Examine your options. For example, if the company is going through a bad patch, could you put your plans on hold for a while? If not and if your ambitions are still gnawing at you this could be a signal for you to go out and try the outside job market.

But if you've gone through the checklist and you're still no wiser as to why you appear to have come up against a glass ceiling, the next area to explore is whether you have communicated your aim properly. Do the powers that be realise that you have got your eyes on a seat on the board? Have you transmitted the message upwards properly? Have you followed it up? If not, then get onto it straight away and follow the steps in Parts 2 and 3.

You have now arrived at the point where you have eliminated the usual reasons for failing to make progress, i.e.:

- the aim is not realisable
- you have not communicated the aim
- you have not completed.

At this stage what you may be left with is one of the assortment of woolly answers that people get when they're pressing for a seat at the top table. Here it is useful to refer back to the case of Lester the chartered accountant (page 101). Lester wanted a seat on the board of his company but his managing director skilfully avoiding giving him a direct yes or no. It was always a case of 'wait and see'. The advice we gave Lester was to put a time limit on how long he would wait and see and to be quite firm about acting as soon as the deadline expired. We warned about squandering away long periods of time waiting for promotions that never seem to arrive.

In summary, don't make it your life's work trying to penetrate glass ceilings, because even if you succeed it can take years. Take our word for it:

- glass ceilings are real
- there are plenty of other companies – companies where you won't find glass ceilings.

....................................................................

# CAN YOU HANDLE A TOP JOB?

CASE STUDY: WILL

As part of the company's management succession plan, Will spent a year understudying the logistics director up to the date of his retirement. Will then stepped into his former boss's shoes and, along with the directorship, his salary was increased by £10k per annum and he became eligible for a number of attractive directors' perks, including share options and a top of the range company car.

Six months into the job, however, Will found himself struggling. He was getting it in the neck from the managing director because of the company's failure to keep delivery promises while at the same time he was being expected to operate with an ever ageing transport fleet. Older trucks meant more breakdowns which meant, in turn, more irate customers on the phone – it was all a vicious circle as far as Will could see, yet the managing director seemed totally unsympathetic and only intent on giving Will a hard time.

Recently the pressure started to get to Will. He found he wasn't sleeping and his wife is now insisting he sees the family doctor because he has become irritable at home. What's the answer, Will wonders – he can't afford to give the job up because on the strength of his increased salary he moved up the housing market and took on bigger mortgage commitments. Yet he can't see himself putting up with these levels of stress much longer – not without his health really suffering. The funny part about it

is that when he was understudying his predecessor, Will had no qualms at all about taking on
director level responsibilities.

There are two advantages to being promoted
into a top job internally:

- you are in familiar surroundings
- the company will be more supportive in
  the period when there is most risk (the
  period at the beginning). Will may be
  getting harsh words but at least his job
  isn't under threat (not yet).

Contrast this with the position of externally
recruited candidates to top jobs, who will soon
be shown the door if they fail to perform.

What Will's case illustrates is the world of
difference between aspiring to top jobs and
actually doing them. We can sympathise with
Will because many of us have been in his
position and what we would probably tell him
to do is tough it out.

Unfortunate though it may seem, the honest answer to the question 'Can you handle a
top job?' is 'You won't know until you try'.
The acid test is in the doing and, up to that
point, you won't really know whether you've
put yourself beyond your level of competence
or not.

Most of us have to look no further than our
own experience to find cases of people who
are perfectly capable in middle management
roles but who struggle when they get promoted into top jobs. The difficulty then is
what to do with them. Clearly they can't carry
on in the top job because too much is at stake,
but neither can they revert to their old job
because the position has been filled.

Years ago failed top managers could look

forward to being shunted sideways into jobs specially created for them but, in today's downsized, slim-line world, soft landings along these lines are rarely available. The more likely outcome is the short, sharp exit treatment in one form or other.

The object of this little lesson in the realities of life at the top is not to be depressing. Rather, what we want to point out to you is this:

- the risk inherent in any move into a top job
- that the riskiest period is at the start
- if you are ambitious you have to take the risk
- at the same time you have to examine the consequences of the job not working out (it could happen): not least you need to examine the financial consequences for you and anyone dependent on you.

In the last section of this part we are going to take a look at structuring your package so that you will have some cushioning if the worst should come to the worst. Executive vulnerability is a real issue these days and you ignore it at your peril. The higher you go, the further and the harder you can fall.

Going back to Will for a moment, taking on a bigger mortgage before he settled into his new job clearly put pressure on him and this was a definite mistake on his part. The time to start enjoying the fruits of a promotion is when you are happy in your own mind that you have passed the test of competence, i.e. when the riskiest period is behind you.

GOLDEN RULE 16

Take account of risk.

........................................................

# HANDLING POLITICS

Politics is a subject all on its own, but as a rule the higher you go up the ladder in a company, the more likely it is that you will have to steer your path through conflicting interest groups. At worst you could find your path to the top blocked by an opposing interest group so, nothing to do with your company's ability to promote you or your value to them, you don't move forward because someone doesn't want you to.

Telling you to avoid politics at the top is a bit like telling you to stand naked in water without getting wet and this brings us to our first subject – patronage. For most of us, we find our way into top jobs because someone believes in us sufficiently to keep promoting us. The chances are that the someone concerned has also been a role model for us during our time with the company and we feel a proper sense of gratitude. Take Paul as an example.

CASE STUDY: PAUL

Paul has risen through the ranks of a large manufacturing company with the support and guidance of Max, the production director. Paul is now being considered for a seat on the board but his appointment is opposed by Hugh, the

> sales director. Hugh sees Paul as in Max's pocket:
> someone who will go with Max on all issues –
> meaning sales' interests will be compromised.

Practically all organisations are broken into rival camps that spend much of their time at loggerheads. Sometimes these camps form around personalities with the bonding provided by allegiance and dispensation of patronage. Sometimes the camps are functional (the classic works versus sales situation in manufacturing companies is a good example – the bonding here is common outlook/ shared experience reinforced by the company's own organisational structure). Occasionally camps can centre around the espousal of a certain principle or idea. For example, 'the best way forward' is the focus point for some camps – expansionists versus conservationists (those who want to go for growth versus those who feel the company is already overborrowed).

Steering round conflicting interest groups by standing apart from them is hardly a plausible alternative. You are sales or you are works; you are one of Max's people or you are one of Hugh's; and you will have principles and ideas which you have aired from time to time (unless you are completely colourless, of course – in which case you are hardly likely to be suitable for a top job) and, not least in this consideration of opposing interest groups, there is the possibility you have made a few powerful enemies as you have climbed the corporate ladder. These enemies could be poised to strike at you as you seek to put your foot on the top rung.

With politics and opposition our advice is to deal with the reality of the situation. When your name is in the hat for a top job run through the following checklist.

## When you are in the running for a top job

- Where is the opposition to your promotion likely to come from (hazard a guess)?

- Who are your supporters? [In Paul's case this will be Max.]

- Speak to your supporters. Voice your concern about opposition. See if your supporters agree.

- Examine ways in which the opposition could be pre-empted. [For example, could Max talk it through with Hugh first? Could he offer a trade off, e.g. Hugh drops his opposition to Paul in return for Max supporting one of Hugh's pet schemes?] Face the fact that this might not be possible. [Max may not be prepared to go with the idea]

- Examine the alternatives. [For example, could Max talk to the chief executive with a view to getting him to steam-roller Hugh's opposition?]

With the reality of politics and the potential for powerful interest groups blocking your path to promotion comes the possibility that what you are attempting to do may not be realisable. This will be particularly the case where the opposition faction is in the ascendancy (the signs should be apparent).

A further difficulty is that you may not be told the real reason for not getting your promotion. The fact that there has been opposition from certain quarters may be concealed from you because all the discussion has gone on behind closed doors. Even your supporter(s) may feel bound by the rules of collective responsibility to withhold the truth from you.

CASE STUDY: TERRENCE

'The MD told me the board had decided not to offer me a directorship because the company's poor trading performance would make it difficult to justify to the shareholders. I knew full well that the personnel director had put the kiss of death on me. She and I have never hit it off and increasingly she has got the ear of the MD.'

But, just as politics can sometimes work against us, they can equally work in our favour. The Max in our lives can facilitate our move up the ladder and, if our faction is in the ascendancy, it will be to our advantage.

| **GOLDEN RULE 17** |

Face up to the reality of politics.

# NEGOTIATING THE PACKAGE

Congratulations. You've received your promotion into a top job, you have achieved your big ambition and everything seems hunky dory – that is, until you find out about the package. Suddenly your smile turns into a frown.

CASE STUDY: HELENA

'I finally made it onto the board of management but the salary increase I got was way below my expectations. My further disappointment was when I was told I had to keep my middle management grade car until it came up for renewal in two years' time.'

What do you do in these situations? You want the promotion but you don't like the package. But how do you accept one without the other? And if you start quibbling about the pay and perks don't you run the risk of having the whole deal taken away from you?

The key to understanding how to proceed in these cases is to realise that what you are trying to do is treat two aims as one:

- getting the promotion
- getting the package right.

Remember what we said about taking your aims one at a time? Helena has got her promotion so, great, she has achieved her first aim and she can tick that one off. But now she has to get working on her second aim (getting the package right) and here we would refer her back to what we said about going for pay increases on pages 77–81. There are a few little warnings though.

## Asking for a pay increase

- Leave it for a while. Get yourself through that risky period at the start of all top jobs. Don't complicate matters by putting in for a pay increase at a time when your performance is still under scrutiny.

- Allow for the fact that your company may still be wanting to see you perform in your new job before bringing your pay up to the appropriate level.

- Watch what you are basing your expectations on. Comparators are a big problem with top jobs – as we shall see in our next case study on Jeremy.

- In Helena's case, letting her old car run out its normal life makes good sense. To do otherwise (trade in a perfectly serviceable vehicle) is wasteful. The mistake here is to start thinking that your 'right' takes precedence over the company's duty to manage its assets efficiently and prudently. As part of top management, concerns such as these are just as much yours.

## When an outsider earns more than you

Now we'll turn to another knotty little problem for the newly promoted: what to do when the company appoints someone from outside into a comparable job to yours but at a much higher salary. You are both new to your jobs so it can't be said the difference in money reflects the other person's performance – and, as this seems to happen such a lot, does it simply illustrate that companies are prepared to pay more to people who come in from outside? If so, is this taking advantage of the internally promoted?

CASE STUDY: JEREMY

'I recently got a seat on the board of my company. My salary went up by £12k, I got a nice new top of the range car and I became eligible for some very attractive perks (including share options). In short I was perfectly happy with my deal – until Malcolm came along. Malcolm is the new director in charge of advertising and public relations. He was headhunted from a firm in the City and put on a salary almost double my own. Just to rub further salt into the wound, he was also paid a £20,000 golden hello. Since my responsibilities cover all the operational side of the business, about 85% of the personnel we employ reports through to me so, try though I did, I could see no justification for why Malcolm with his staff of ten should be given such preferential treatment. Frankly I feel livid.

If it's any consolation to Jeremy he is not alone in his experience of seeing reputed high-fliers brought in on much higher salaries and with all sorts of inducements to encourage them to join and, like Jeremy, people on the receiving end of such experiences usually feel hard done by. Whereas previously they were quite happy with their lots, they now feel angry and frustrated because they see no reason for their less favourable treatment other than the fact they have come up through the ranks. Not unreasonably they ask themselves: is this the way the company rewards loyalty and long service? Is this how they give recognition to us for all the hard work we have put in over the years?

In recruiting top executive talent on the outside job market, the packages companies offer have to reflect two very hard facts of life:

- the going rate for the skills and experience they wish to procure. Simple supply and demand economics apply here: the scarcer the skill and experience the more they are going to have to pay.

For example, in Jeremy's industry it could be that top advertising and public relations practitioners command a higher market rate than directors in charge of operations. If so, there is nothing Jeremy can do about it

- what it will take to entice the person they wish to recruit.

Into this second category come considerations such as:

- risk – in today's uncertain world, moving from one company to another is always a plunge into the unknown. Who knows if it will work out? And why take the risk unless there is some money in it?

- compensation – moving jobs means loss of employment rights and loss of service. Not least it means loss of whatever track record and reputation the candidate has built up with his or her present employer (the lifelong interview has to start all over again). Pension rights come into this, too: moving jobs usually means forfeiting something on the superannuation front

- disruption – this is especially the case where relocation is required: where wives' or husbands' jobs are affected; where children's educations are disrupted; where domestic routines and arrangements have to be restructured.

Is there anything you notice about this last list of bullet points? None of these concerns figure for internally promoted people such as Jeremy:

- They are in familiar surroundings: they know the culture of the company, they know the politics and their networks are in place. They also know the directions they can turn in when things get rough.

- The company will be generally more supportive of them. They will normally be given more time to prove themselves.

- If things do go wrong the company will be more inclined towards sympathy. They will be seen as 'one of the family' and more will be done for them than it would for an externally recruited candidate.

The bottom line for Jeremy is this: would he be prepared to uproot himself and take a big risk? If so, the outside job market is there waiting for him and there is nothing to stop him putting himself forward. If all works out for him then doubtless he too would be offered a big package and all sorts of inducements to tempt him out of his tree.

But really what this is proving is:

- you don't get the market price unless you go out and stand in the marketplace
- no one will pay you golden hellos and enticement premiums for staying where you are.

## REDUCING YOUR EXPOSURE TO RISK

Having established that internal promotees are at far less risk than candidates recruited on the outside job market, there is still the possibility that your promotion doesn't work out for you and, earlier on in this part, we advised you to have a few contingency plans in mind for what you would do if the worst ever came to the worst.

CASE STUDY: NEIL

'When I took on responsibility for the Scottish operation, my boss and I acknowledged that I might be taking a step too far. Still, the Scottish operation was without a manager and I felt the experience would be good for me even if the job didn't work out long term, so on that basis we both decided that I should give it a try. Part of the deal was that for six months I would have the option of returning to my old job in Liverpool and, for the same period, I would not be required to relocate (the company would pay my hotel bills).'

Neil's situation is slightly unusual in that:

- the possibility of the job not working out can be openly discussed
- the company is prepared to let him give it a try
- his old job will still be available to him.

Depending on the circumstances and your relationship with your company and your boss you may be able to negotiate an agreement like Neil's: you agree to try the job and the company agrees to give you a lifeline in the event of things not turning out in the way you both hoped. But the likelihood is that you won't be in Neil's situation because:

- you will have every confidence that you can do the job. It will be something you have aspired to and something you have few or any qualms about. As in Will's case, the difficulties, if they arise at all, will only arise after you have spent a little time sitting in the hot seat and not before

- the company will have every confidence in you and that is the basis on which they will be offering you the job. For certain, they wouldn't be putting their money on you if they felt you might fail.

In these circumstances it is not only difficult to open up discussions on 'what happens if I find I can't do the job ...', it simply doesn't occur to you because you don't see the need. So, if six, nine or twelve months down the track you have to put your hand up and say 'Sorry, this isn't for me', the probability is there won't be any lifelines for you. Someone else will be doing your old job and the prospect of bumping a whole line of people back downwards certainly won't appeal.

You may elicit some sympathy from your boss. Your boss may even try to persuade you to give it a bit longer. Your company may indeed be one of these enlightened organisations who offer professional counselling or support to people in your position. But again, the likelihood is that your throwing in the towel will be greeted by a stunned silence.

The company may be able to come up with an alternative and, with this in mind, it pays not to leave matters to the point where they become desperate. It will be much better for you if you can flag up to your company that you are struggling with the job but that you will carry on for the time being in the hope that, between the two of you, you will be able to arrive at a solution. Two tales from human resources directors illustrate the point.

**CAROLE:**

'Bearing in mind we are talking about someone running a key part in this business and earning more than I am, he came into my office one morning, sat with his head in his hands and said he couldn't go on. We ended up putting him on garden leave, then, thankfully, he put his notice in. We were very relieved he did, I can tell you.'

**SEA-JIN:**

'The first we knew about Bernard not being able to handle the job was when he put a sick note in laying him off work for two months with stress. "We're all b … well stressed," was the managing director's reaction. "What right has he got to take two months off on full pay?" The final outcome was we dismissed Bernard on grounds of medical incapacity. The MD was quite adamant we wouldn't have him back in the company under any circumstances.'

What's interesting about these stories is that:

- in both cases the individuals concerned probably struggled in silence for some time
- because of their actions, they totally lost any sympathy that the company might have had for them.

So what should you do if you find yourself in a situation like Will's, on page 133? The first piece of advice is don't resign. Even though flogging on may be painful to you, quitting and walking out with nothing when your notice expires really is a case of jumping out of the frying pan into the fire.

The first step when you find yourself in a job you can't do is to explore the alternatives and, if you come clean with your company there is more than an even chance that you will have them on your side. At this juncture they may ask you to try the job a bit longer – in which case you should go along with the suggestion and give it your best shot.

At the end of this part you will find a question that deals with viewing alternative job offers (what to do if the offer is a down-wards move).

This brings us next to where you and your company have to face the fact that there is nowhere for you to go.

You may be fortunate enough to have a clause in your contract (a so-called golden parachute) that guarantees you a soft landing in the form of a big hand-out if you should find your career in a state of free fall. But for most of us, apart from our contractual period of notice, we don't have a lot to fall back on when we find ourselves in these situations. Our exits are something we have to negotiate.

## Arriving at settlement

To suggest to someone who has just come a cropper in a top job that they have bargaining power sounds a contradiction. Yet consider this: your company now has the problem of what to do with you. You're not performing in the job but you're not resigning either so this leaves them with the problem of having to make the moves to terminate your contract. What will be weighing on their minds is:

- potential litigation – in the UK this means the possibility of having to defend an unfair dismissal claim in front of an Employment Tribunal (something most employers don't look forward to)

- image – how will other senior managers view it if poor old Will is pushed out with a mean deal?

- damage limitation – what if Will has got some knowledge in his head which could be useful to a competitor?

These are all compulsions on employers to come to amicable agreements with top executives who have to go. This, in other words, is your silent bargaining power.

So given the situation you are in, what should you be looking for in terms of a settlement with your company?

## Factors to take into account in a settlement

- You will have to find another (comparable) job and the higher up the ladder you are, the harder this is going to be for you. Your age comes into this, too: if you are 55 the outside job market will be less receptive to you than if you are 35. There are also your skills to consider: if your skills are specialised it will be much harder to find a niche for them. These considerations form the basis of a guestimate of how long it will take you to find another job: six weeks? six months? A year? From this guestimate you can work out the monetary part of the compensation deal.

- You will lose your fringe benefits: your car, your medical insurance and anything else you are entitled to. A straight monetary calculation of what these benefits are worth is possible (based again on a guestimate of how long it will take you to find another job). Alternatively, your company may be prepared to give you the car or sell it to you at a knock-down price. Similarly they may be able to buy you into the medical plan for a forward period.

- If you are in the usual final salary occupational pension scheme, you will find your pension entitlements suffer. Ask a pensions' adviser to help you do the sums, but perhaps the company could see its way to enhancing the transfer values available to you or making a one-off payment into a personal pension plan?

In coming to an agreement with your company on the terms of your departure you may need to take the following into account:

- You may disagree with the company how long it is going to take you to find another job. Their view may be more optimistic than yours and what you could do here is negotiate a pay-as-you-go scheme in place of a one one-off lump sum. They pay you an agreed figure, say monthly, in exchange for you furnishing them with proof you are still out of work. If you find yourself in a less well paid (stop-gap) job you could equally furnish them with proof of your earnings and the compensation would then be based on the difference between your old salary

and what you are getting paid in the
stop-gap job.

• Even if you are subject to a contractual
restraint, your company may still, as part
of the agreement, want you to affirm that
you will not use confidential information
without their agreement.

• Your company may insist on paying you
by instalments. This gives them a rein-
check on you if you should misbehave in
any way.

• Your company may want you to sign a
document to say that you accept the deal
as being in full and final settlement of
any claims you may have against them.
In the UK this deal may be done under
the auspices of the government's
Arbitration and Conciliation Service
(ACAS).

---

**GOLDEN RULE 18**

Never resign.

---

...........................................................................

## QUESTIONS AND ANSWERS

### Where the alternative is a step backwards

**Q** I am in a situation where I was promoted
into a top job a year ago but found I couldn't
cope with the pressures, mainly due to lack of
experience, i.e. I took a step too far and paid

the price. The company have been very good to me but now they have come up with an offer of alternative employment which isn't to my liking. The job is in another part of the group but in terms of both the responsibilities and the package, it is at a much lower level than the job I had prior to my promotion. I am inclined to say no but I realise that in doing so I run the risk of alienating my company's support. What do you suggest I do in these circumstances?

**A** Thriving in companies means having the ability to move round in them: upwards, sideways and – yes – occasionally downwards. The fact that you are still there, still going, is all that matters. The opportunity to come bouncing back will present itself soon.

## TICK YOUR PROGRESS

✓ Don't automatically feel it's you when the doors to top jobs don't open for you.

✓ Smashing through glass ceilings is difficult. Don't make it your life's work.

✓ Acknowledge that moving into top jobs means taking risks. Be ready for things not working out.

✓ Don't resign if the going gets tough.

✓ Use the politics in your company to advance your progress.

✓ Don't let the package on offer get in the way of accepting promotion. Take your aims one at a time.

✓ Don't let your vision be clouded by envy.
Don't let the big packages offered to
external candidates sour your view of the
company.

## Part five

# FLAT, FRAGMENTED AND SMALL COMPANIES

**I**ncreasingly in the modern world people find their career paths either non-existent or truncated. This can be explained by three trends of recent times:

- delayering – companies take out levels of management to cut costs, resulting in the familiar flat organisation: one in which the next step up has been taken away

- decentralising – companies opt for simpler, more devolved systems of management. The result is larger companies broken down into small autonomous units where career prospects are limited by the unit's size

- increasing numbers of small firms where again the prospects are limited by size.

In this part we will look at the special challenge that flat companies, fragmented companies and small companies present to people in careers. We will pay particular attention to the following topics:

- within these structures, what's realisable and what isn't

- the potential for lateral job extension; the opportunity to broaden your skills and experience and add to your value

- pay progression: how small and unstructured organisations often pay good salaries; how silent bargaining power can be brought to bear

- visibility: the problem of projecting

yourself across organisational boundaries; how to get your face known and network in fragmented companies.

...................................................................................

# PROFILING COMPANIES WHERE THERE ARE NO OBVIOUS CAREER PATHS

If you can cast your mind back to our first part, you will recall that we looked at a case study about three business graduates (Laura, Mike and Andrea) – three bright young people who all had similar career aspirations but who were working in very different types of organisations.

First there was Laura, who was in a traditional big company where the onward movement of her career seemed to require little input from her end. Next there was Mike, who was stuck in a rut through no fault of his own and largely because his company had opted for a decentralised structure. Mike's problem was how to get himself in line for promotions that were happening elsewhere in the company. And there was Andrea, who was working for a small firm of stockbrokers where the money was good but where the chances of promotion were practically nil.

## Small companies

We used Laura, Mike and Andrea to illustrate the importance of profiling your company – examining its capacity to provide you with the kind of career you want and highlighting situations where you may be pursuing career aims that are not realisable however hard you try. In Andrea's case, for example, if she pressed for promotion in her small firm she would hit resistance because the next step up would involve a partnership. Because Andrea has interpreted things correctly she has realised that this is unlikely (at least for the foreseeable future); hence, she knows that if she wants to get on at the pace she has set herself, she will need to explore the outside job market at some point – a larger stock-broker perhaps. What she will certainly not be doing is wasting her effort on her present employers. Nice people they may be, but they can't deliver what Andrea wants.

It is a mistake however, to write off small firms completely and the following two case studies will help to illustrate this.

## CASE STUDY: EDWARD

'I am a management accountant and I work in a small company where I have acquired experience and skills that I would never have acquired in a bigger firm. I am involved in all aspects of running the business and I am given a very free hand. Recently the company decided to purchase a new computer and I was put in charge of the project. With my old firm, anything to do with computers would have been dealt with by the IT manager. I would never have been given so much as a look in.'

Small companies are like this. Willing pairs of hands have all sorts of tasks placed into them and lines between management functions are blurred. What's even better is that there's often great scope for extending jobs in small companies by simply saying when the opportunity arises, 'I'll do that: leave it to me.' Most small firms will be perfectly happy to let you get on with it. In Edward's case, his cv will benefit greatly from this extension to his skills and experience into IT and he will find that he is far more marketable in a world where breadth of skills and experience commands a premium. So the message is: if you work in a small company use the opportunity it offers.

CASE STUDY: INGRID

'The small company I work for has been in business for three years. In that time its annual turnover has grown from £500,000 to £6½ million and we are forecasting sales of £9 million next year. In my short time here I have acquired a lot of product knowledge and, with the company's growth, I rate my future prospects as excellent

Small companies don't necessarily stay small companies and, with the visibility that comes with working in small companies (everyone knows everyone else), the chances for promotion in these high-growth situations are very good indeed (growing with the company). Of particular importance to you in profiling a small company is its top management. Are they Go-for-Growth Joes or are they Steady Eddies? There is nothing wrong with Steady Eddies except the company will probably stay a small company for some time (longer than you may be prepared to put up with).

## Fragmented companies

Mike's company is fragmented. His aims to a large extent do seem realisable – the company is big enough and the promotion jobs are there. The problem for him is that, because of the company's decentralised structure, he can't get his face in the frame when the opportunities arise. The difficulty Mike has, therefore, is one of visibility; we will be looking at how to overcome visibility difficulties in fragmented companies in the final section of this part (pages 170–3).

## Flat companies

Flat companies are strange animals in that, pre-delayering, the career paths used to be there. As a consequence, people who work in flat companies take the view that something they once had has been taken away from them and this affects their perceptions. Sometimes these perceptions are reinforced by the utterances of higher management.

CASE STUDY: RALPH

'When I took this job it was made plain to me that the company had a flat structure and the chances of moving up the ladder were practically nil. My boss told me that after three years I ought to be thinking about moving on.'

Perhaps this is a case of being painfully honest – and there's nothing wrong with that – but from a career progression point of view are flat companies all bad? Indeed, is there anything in the make-up of flat companies that makes them exploitable from a self-managed career point of view.

## CASE STUDY: MEL

'My company is made up of four product divisions. Previously the management structure consisted of the managing director at the top with four divisional managers reporting to him. Beneath the divisional managers came the sales, production and distribution managers for each product group and I am the distribution manager of the paints division. The company, incidentally, is part of a group.

'Following catastrophic trading results, the edict came down from head office to cut costs dramatically. The chief executive actually specified that the divisional managers would have to go – meaning that in future people like me would report directly to the MD. This I took as bad news because my divisional manager was due to retire in eighteen months and it had been indicated to me that I was in line to step into his shoes. As I saw it, my career path had been wiped out with one blow.

'After the divisional managers had gone, the next question was what to do with their responsibilities. Because the MD had no inclination to get involved in day-to-day operational problems he decided to delegate most of them, meaning I now find that I am completely running my own show. Decisions I previously referred upwards are decisions I take myself. While I would still prefer to have the divisional manager's job to aspire to (and the extra perks and cash) I recognise that I am gaining in terms of my experience and skills. Some day I am sure this will stand me in good stead.'

Mel's tale of empowerment illustrates that good can come from these seemingly bad situations although sometimes the good may have to be coaxed, e.g. if Mel's MD had taken the divisional managers' responsibilities under his own wing then the suggestion to delegate them might have had to come from Mel. The pay and perks? Perhaps they would be best left till when the company's trading performance starts to pick up again, i.e. when the effects of the cost-cutting measures start to work through. Mel could perhaps then incorporate an improvement in his package into his aims.

---

**GOLDEN RULE 19**

Seek to empower yourself.

---

There are other opportunities within flat companies. Take the case of Shelley.

CASE STUDY: SHELLEY

'My career path in the old organisation would have gone from account manager (my present job), to area manager, to regional controller. There are no area managers any more so I find myself in the position of being offered a regional controller's job with an absolutely fantastic increase in my salary and an elevation two grades up the scale with my choice of company car.'

What Shelley is witnessing is taking two steps up the ladder in one go. In flat companies the promotions may be harder to get, but when they do come they tend to be big jumps.

In passing, it should be mentioned that some flat companies have recognised the problem they are giving to people in careers and have responded with all kinds of job enrichment and empowerment programmes. If you work in one of these enlightened companies, then great, but do remember always to keep to your own agenda. Don't ever let it escape your attention if the promotion opportunity you are hankering after is either not there or in very short supply (difficult to realise).

## ADDING TO YOUR VALUE BY BROADENING YOUR EXPERIENCE AND SKILLS

The concerns that enlightened flat companies are having and that we have just noted are not entirely born out of a sense of altruism. Companies that have gone down the delayering route have found that one of the unfortunate side-effects of not providing people with careers is that they leave and, in these cases, of course, it is always the best people who go:

- those who are keen and want promotion
- those who are snapped up by other companies as soon as they set foot on the outside job market.

These anxieties are not just confined to flat companies – small companies and fragmented companies face the same difficulty, too.

CASE STUDY: WASIM

'Our big problem is retaining people of the right calibre. We pay them good salaries, but because we are a company with only twenty employees, we can't make them all into senior managers and directors. Sadly, we have to face the fact that people use us to gain skills and experience then go off and get a good job with someone else.'

This awareness of retention difficulties is interesting and it is nowhere more prevalent than the kind of organisations we are looking at in this part.

- small organisations (or small because they are fragmented), where people are thin on the ground and where individuals quickly become key players

- delayered and downsized organisations, where people are thinner on the ground than they used to be and where more and more work is concentrated into fewer and fewer pairs of hands.

In both situations someone putting in their notice can often induce a state of near panic. Going back to Mel on page 162 as an example, if Mel left it would impact directly on the top level of management in his company – that is, the MD. The MD would soon find himself embroiled in the nitty gritty of the paint division distribution department and we can only hazard a guess that this would be something he would go to great lengths to avoid.

What we are seeing here is that people in small companies, flat companies and fragmented companies add value to themselves because their employers are vulnerable and under pressure. In consequence their silent bargaining power becomes immense.

## The art of the possible

What won't do any good in these companies, of course, is asking them to provide you with what they can't deliver, e.g. promotions to senior management jobs. But where you will score is with aims that are realisable, notably the extension of your bank of skills and experience and, as a consequence, the extension of your responsibilities in the way that Edward did back on page 159.

The prospect that is opening up for you here is to write your own job description and indulge in a bit of job creation by the good old-fashioned method of empire building.

Situations ripe for exploitation are where:

- job boundaries are flexible
- people are working under pressure
- offers to take on more responsibility will be welcome.

CASE STUDY: KATE

'I started here as company secretary, then, because the MD wanted to free her hands to look at acquisitions and developing retail outlets, I took over responsibility for buying and accounts. As we grew, so human resources became an issue and we recruited a personnel officer who was put under me. Now I have added sales to my portfolio – mainly because it has become a hot potato and the MD doesn't feel she has time to give it the attention it needs.

.........................................................................

# EXPLOITING THE PAY POTENTIAL OF UNSTRUCTURED COMPANIES

To recap, whether your pay ambitions are realisable or not largely depends on two factors:

- your company's ability to deliver the package you want
- your value to your company as expressed through your silent bargaining power.

With flat companies, fragmented companies and small companies we have seen just how conditioned they are to attaching a high value to key people. But what about the other half of the equation – their ability to deliver on pay? How do they fare on this front?

For the answer to this question we need to look at the difference in the way structured and unstructured companies view and fix salaries.

Given that they are trading at a reasonable level, large structured companies tend to see their salaries in terms of certain comparators, notably:

- going rates within their area and trade (ensuring that they are competitive). To this end you will find that the human resources or remuneration specialists in these organisations devote a lot of time to studying pay surveys and/or picking up information about pay levels from their grapevines

- differentials – keeping peer groups at more or less the same level; maintaining differentials between different levels in the hierarchy.

The result, very often, is that these structured organisations have salary scales or bands within which excellence and effort can be rewarded. Annual pay increments ('the rations') are added to these scales or bands but scope to move outside them is usually limited because of the knock-on effect on differentials and the problems this can cause. Higher up the hierarchy there may be no scales or bands as such but some sort of formal or informal benchmarking system will be in operation so that salaries of senior managers will have a rational relationship with one another. Contrast this with flat companies, fragmented companies and small companies where comparators are:

- less evident because there are fewer people or, as in the case of flat companies, the differentials between levels in the hierarchy are so big that there is more scope for flexibility

- likely to be subordinated to other, more immediate, considerations.

For an illustration of what we mean by the second, read Gemma and Russell's case study.

### CASE STUDY: GEMMA AND RUSSELL

Russell runs a small and very profitable company which offers a metallurgical quality control and testing service to the casting and forging industries. He owns the company outright which employs twenty-five people.

Gemma is Russell's number two. She is a high-flying materials science graduate in her early thirties and she has been with the company five years.

Russell pays Gemma an extremely good salary, much better than she would get working as a metallurgist anywhere else. Russell views his treatment of Gemma as a good investment. Not only does she bring a good intelligent input into the business, she also takes half the burden off Russell's shoulders as far as out-of-hours calls from customers are concerned. In fact, if Gemma left, Russell would soon find himself working six or sometimes seven days a week, with no holidays.

Gemma's value to Russell has a very personal dimension to it and this is the case in a lot of unstructured organisations. If Gemma wasn't there Russell's life would be painful in the extreme. Seeing that he owns the company and can please himself how he spends his money, paying Gemma a good salary makes eminent sense. The least of Russell's concerns is comparators. The fact that he's paying Gemma 50% more than the going rate for metallurgists in the area has little relevance to him.

Here we have a situation where:

- the company's ability to pay is not subject to any of the usual constraints
- the employee's silent bargaining power is substantial.

The result, not surprisingly, is that Gemma, in common with a lot of key people in unstructured organisations, makes very good money indeed. However, there is a downside, which is that when, for career advancement reasons, Gemma has to leave Russell's company she will find from a pay point of view that the outside market has little or nothing to offer her. (You will find a question at the end of this part that deals with this situation.)

........................................................................

# FRAGMENTED COMPANIES: THE PROBLEM OF VISIBILITY

Visibility, putting your face in the corporate frame, has few problems in small companies where everyone knows everyone else and where the figure at the top usually has a direct and very personal relationship with every member of the staff. The same is true of flat companies, where visibility is facilitated by the structure itself. If there are fewer levels of management, the view from the top to the bottom is across a shorter span. If you go back to Mel on page 162, he now reports directly to the managing director, hence his corporate visibility is enhanced over what it used to be.

Visibility, as we saw earlier, links in with networking and particularly with networking beyond your immediate circle (your immediate peer group or your immediate boss). Accordingly, in small companies and flat companies the opportunities for developing internal networks are extremely good and lack of visibility and networks tend not to be the reason why people don't get on.

Difficulty with visibility and networking does, however, arise in fragmented, loosely strung together organisations, and such organisations sometimes have the added disadvantage of being geographically scattered. Furthermore, their head offices are often remote and consist of little beside the chief executive's staff and the personnel involved in consolidating the accounts. Though lip service may be paid to developing people's careers, the reality is that little is done because the machinery doesn't exist (e.g. there is no corporate human resources function to oversee things). As Mike, one of our three business graduates was finding, people's careers in fragmented companies tend to be confined to the tiny part of the organisation they work in. If the opportunities to move forward are in other parts of the company the chances are they won't even hear about them and communicating their aims to their bosses may not do a lot of good because their bosses may be in exactly the same boat as they are in. People who can move round in these loosely strung together organisations tend to be people who are extremely good at networking and visibility. Frequently they are people who can display a little inventiveness and initiative.

The following three case studies show how three individuals have tackled the challenge of visibility in fragmented organisations by taking matters into their own hands.

### CASE STUDY: ABLA

'The company is sponsoring me to do an MBA and it struck me that across the group there must be a number of people doing the same thing. With my boss's permission I sent out an e-mail to the various locations to see who was out there and, in all, I had twenty-five responses. As a result, we set up our own special interest group – we regularly swap information about projects, compare notes and two weeks ago we held our first conference. For the first time I can say I have a genuine insight into what other companies in the group do and I have contacts in all of them.'

## CASE STUDY: ROBERT

'A number of us in the office play tennis and we hit on the idea of having a company-wide tennis tournament. My boss kindly agreed to have a word with the group chief executive, who gave his blessing and donated a prize. The company also agreed to pay for the venue (a commercial sports complex) and, by advertising the tournament across the group, we got over forty entrants. The tournament was a great success. I didn't win but in the socialising between games I got to know a lot of people from other parts of the company and I have kept in touch with them ever since.'

## CASE STUDY: GABY

'I am a buyer and it has always occurred to me what tremendous buying power the group could exert if we negotiated with some suppliers collectively. I put up a case to my MD and with his approval I made contact with my opposite numbers in other companies in the group. The result was a working party that eventually turned into a buying consortium (we have already saved the group in excess of £100,000). From my point of view the most valuable part of the exercise is the contacts I have made. The other buyers and I now regularly pick one another's brains and exchange of information about suppliers is a daily event.'

Neither Abla, Robert nor Gaby set up their cross-group networks with a view to advancing their careers. Yet as a result of their initiatives they are now known across a much wider spectrum of their organisations than they were previously and, as a consequence, the chances of them picking up on interesting opportunities have been considerably enhanced. Two further points to note with these case studies are:

- the way Abla, Robert and Gaby took care to keep their bosses on their sides
- the visibility they have created is visibility that associated them with good things: respectively, striving to get qualifications, sporting competition and saving the company money.

The message on visibility in fragmented organisations is: see it as a challenge and tackle it by being inventive and proactive. If you work in a decentralised organisation, ask yourself if there is anything you can do along the Abla, Robert and Gaby lines?

| GOLDEN RULE 20 |

Be inventive and proactive.

......................................................................

## QUESTIONS AND ANSWERS

### Job extension: doing more for the same pay

Q I work in a small firm and, yes, I see the potential for extending my job by volunteering myself for additional responsibilities, but this strikes me as playing right into my directors' hands. They would be no better pleased than to see me taking on more and more work for no extra pay. Why should I do this? Isn't it a case of letting them take advantage of me?

**A** We would put it another way. The fact that, in common with most principals of small firms, your directors are compliant when it comes to you extending your job is something you should see as an advantage. You can add to your value and step up your silent bargaining power, which means more strength to your elbow when you come to realising your aims. Included in your aims of course will be getting the right rate of pay for the responsibilities you control. Contrast this approach with going to your directors and saying: 'I'll do x, y and z providing you pay me £n extra.' The upshot could well be that they decide to decline your conditional offer and do x, y and z themselves and, as a consequence, your bargaining power stays static. What this is demonstrating is that, to get anything out of a company, you need to put something in first. Trying to do things the other way round doesn't work.

## Well paid and finding it difficult to make the next step in my career

**Q** I suspect I am in a similar position to your example Gemma (page 168). I work as a trouble shooter for a small firm in the construction industry where opportunities for promotion into management are practically nil. Sensing that I was under-achieving, I started applying for jobs then found that, with the various bonuses and allowances I have negotiated for myself, my pay exceeds any of the salaries I am offered and so I now find myself in a flummox as to what to do. I don't want to stagnate but I don't want to move for less money either. Any advice?

**A** First of all, make sure you are not just looking at a small segment of the job market (the jobs you have applied for). You will form a better overview by:

- continuing to make applications (widening the sample)
- talking to a few employment agencies (irrespective of whether you use them or not, they should soon be able to give you a good feel for market rates).

But given that you are in a position where your current job pays more than the jobs you are applying for, there are three things for you to consider:

- are you applying for the right kind of jobs (are you under-reaching?). If so, you should be looking at the next level up
- keep going in the hope of a better-paid job turning up (the diversity of the modern job market helps you here – this is known as 'top-end targeting').
- reflect on the fact that to advance your career you may sometimes have to step sideways or downwards in pay terms – either that or run the risk of stagnating. In other words, the benefits are in the longer term.

## TICK YOUR PROGRESS

...................................

✓ Don't write small companies off. See the opportunities for extending your experience and skills (adding to your value).

✓ Spot small companies in growth situations. See the opportunity to grow with them.

✓ Don't view flat companies as 'all bad'.

✓ Take advantage of opportunities to take on more responsibility. Let empowerment add weight to your silent bargaining power.

✓ Use your silent bargaining power to negotiate a good deal for yourself. See this as something that will be harder to achieve in more structured (larger) organisations.

✓ Take on the challenge of visibility in fragmented companies. Be proactive and find ways of projecting yourself across corporate boundaries.

# THE GOLDEN
# RULES

## Rule 1.
**Be realistic about what your company can offer.**

*Don't knock your head against brick walls by pursuing aims that are not realisable.*

There is no point at all in flogging on year after year with aims that are not realisable in the context of your company. It will lead to under-achievement, frustration and, ultimately, loss of confidence. Before pursuing any ambition check first your company's capacity to deliver.

## Rule 2.
**Master the art of the possible.**

*Don't pursue aims that are too narrow and inflexible. Instead take advantage of what's there.*

In trying to advance your career, there is no joy whatsoever in banging your head on a brick wall year after year. Sooner or later the frustration will get to you, and unless you have a will of cast iron you will end up feeling discouraged and despondent. The art of the possible is ensuring that you don't do this; we have seen two examples already:

- profiling your comany so that you identify any aims that are unrealisable and don't waste your time pursuing them
- being flexible so that you take advantage of the opportunities that are there rather than wait for what you consider to be ideal situations to materialise (you could be waiting a long time).

Mastering the art of the possible is an important part of thriving because it is the key to making sure your ideas don't end up as pie in the sky.

## Rule 3.
### Spot the danger signs.

*Know when your job may be at risk. Take immediate steps if it is.*

Few occupations these days can be viewed as jobs for life and an important part of career management is not to close your mind off to the possibility of job loss (ever). There are usually a few warning signs of when the redundancy axe is about to descend and you should attune yourself to picking up these signs.

Clearly a company that is always laying people off is not a place on which to base your future.

## Rule 4.
### Manage your own career.

*Don't let others take the decisions for you. Take responsibility for your future directions.*

Over the last twenty years the world of careers has changed out of all recognition:

- Gone, to a great extent, are the nice tidy career paths that once existed in large companies and the pyramid-shaped hierarchies that supported them. Gone, in many cases, are the large companies themselves.

- Today's large companies are more likely to be broken up into small autonomous businesses or profit centres where there are no obvious career paths – and no co-ordination of human resources policies at the centre, either.

- Hierarchies have often been flattened down by taking out levels of management (delayering).

- The steps that once formed part of people's careers are no longer available.

- Small companies proliferate. By definition small companies don't have much to offer in the way of career paths.

The message is this. Having a career today means taking it into your own hands: don't leave it to others to make the decisions for you bcause they won't. The responsibility for moving your career in the direction you want it to go in lies with you and no one else.

## Rule 5.
**Take responsibility for communicating your aims.**

*Make sure your company understands you. Make sure they're not writing you off as someone who has no ambitions.*

As an aspect of managing your own career, you should be in no doubt that the onus rests on you for making your company understand you. The fact that your boss is too busy, too introspect, too indolent, too remote or too anything else is irrelevant. This is your career: it is your job to look after it and steer in the direction you want it to go in. Never leave it to others to manage your career for you. Never leave it to chance either.

## Rule 6.
### Never grouse.

*However badly done by you feel, don't give the impression you're walking round with a chip on your shoulder.*

Grousers are people who complain constantly about their jobs, their companies and the people they work with (including their bosses). No one listens to grousers (not seriously). Grousing therefore achieves little and is largely wasted effort.

Thrivers, in contrast, value their jobs, their companies and their colleagues. They set aims for themselves and seek to achieve their aims by communicating them properly. When they don't get what they want they take stock. What they never do is complain.

## Rule 7.
### Never make threats.

*Don't pursue aims by telling your company you'll leave if you don't get what you want. Let silent bargaining power do the work for you.*

Companies don't take kindly to people who back their demands with threats. Even when they give in, they do so grudgingly and the incident is never completely forgotten.

To impress the company that they are serious about their aims, thrivers use persistence:

- They present their aims clearly.
- They review their aims periodically.

- They re-state their aims when they think it is necessary.
- They put time limits on how long they give their companies and stick to them.

Companies don't need reminding that they run the risk of losing employees whose aims they cannot meet.

## Rule 8.
### Listen to advice and criticism.

*Don't think you know it all. Others can often give you interesting insights on developing your career.*

One of the difficulties in managing your own career is that any view you take of where you are going and what you need to do to achieve your aims is subjective – and herein lie some dangers:

- Your experience (in life terms) may be narrow. This is not just a question of age: for example, people with one-company careers will have narrower life experience than people who have worked in several different places. If your life experience is narrow then there is a danger that you may not be seeing all the options and possibilities open to you.

- Your knowledge of your company may be incomplete. For example, what do you know about your company's board level politics? What appears as a simple decision to you could in reality have all sorts of complications and side issues.

- Your opinion of yourself may not be as others see you. How you view your strengths and weaknesses may be different from what your boss and your colleagues think.

Thrivers listen to advice and criticism. They encourage feedback from the people they work with. They reflect on what they hear and incorporate good points into their ideas. They don't close off this important source of learning about themselves by being difficult to talk to or rejecting comments that are at odds with their own opinions.

Thrivers take positive steps to tap into the knowledge and experience bank of other people, particularly people with wider knowledge and experience than themselves. They use their networks and target people to bounce their ideas off:

- bosses, and anyone else in their companies who can influence their career outcomes (e.g. human resources managers)

- colleagues, especially colleagues who have 'been around'

- in big companies with structured arrangements for career development, people like mentors and counsellors; people who work within the training and development functions.

- anyone in their circle of friends who has experience of business management, in particular anyone who has worked in the human resources management field

- professional contacts (e.g. fellow members of professional associations).

In passing, note that seeking advice and criticism is also a great way of being visible (see Part 3).

## Rule 9.
### Stay credible.

*Make sure your company goes on believing in you. Don't do anything to destroy their acceptance of the messages you are putting across.*

In the business of achieving career aims, a lot depends on your credibility. If your company believes what you are saying, they will attach proper importance to it.

Credibility is important to you. Without it, your company will never take you seriously and communicating your aims won't work.

## Rule 10.
### Give your best to every day.

*Don't allow lapses in your performance to spoil your lifelong interview.*

People who let their companies down, people who only put in effort when it suits them, people who couldn't care less about the quality of their work, are people who don't get on and people who ultimately put their jobs at risk.

Thrivers look after their jobs and make themselves into people their companies value: Notably:

- they don't have off days
- they are 100% reliable: they go back to people when they say they will; they complete their work to targets

- their appearance is always up to scratch
- they don't run down their colleagues and their bosses; if they have any opinions on the people they work with they make sure to keep them to themselves
- they don't blame subordinates for mistakes
- they don't take time off unless it's absolutely necessary; if they are absent, they are meticulous about keeping everyone informed
- the gloss most people save up for interviews is the image they project every day.

Giving every day your best isn't easy. It calls for consistency and application at the highest level. Thrivers make sure they deliver both.

## Rule 11.
**Take every chance to add value to yourself.**

*Opportunities to increase your skills and knowledge should never be missed.*

People who pass up the chance to acquire new skills are people who become narrow. People in both of these categories are on the road to stagnating but, worse still for them, they are subtracting from their value (their value to their own company and to other employers). As a consequence, their bargaining power is weak and they will find it hard to achieve what they want to achieve.

   To thrive in your company – to keep your job safe and to move forward in the way that you want – you need to be ready to say yes to any opportunity to add to your value.

## Rule 12.
### Make yourself visible.

*Don't hide your light under a bushel. Make sure everyone knows you are there.*

People who put themselves in the woodwork achieve nothing. Eventually they stagnate and for good people this is a pity.

Thrivers stay out of the woodwork by making themselves visible:

- They make sure their bosses are aware of their success
- They use their visibility to put the focus on attributes that add to their value.

## Rule 13.
### Don't hold back with giving your time and effort.

*What you get out of your company will reflect what you put in. Don't expect anything unless you give first.*

Asking for a deal 'up front' rarely works. Before companies promote people, give them rises or send them on expensive training courses, they want some track record and evidence of commitment. People who hold back won't meet these criteria. (Remember there are no prizes for those who refuse to run in the race.) Thrivers recognise these facts and get their expectations the right way round:

- They don't try to 'trade' their effort ('I'll do this if you do that'). They give their effort freely and without condition.
- They see the bigger issues and play the long game.

- They never see themselves as being exploited.
- They use their giving to gain them visibility. As a consequence they add value to themselves and boost their silent bargaining power.

## Rule 14.
### Keep the boss on your side.

*Don't do anything to alienate the person you report to. View your boss as your best ally.*

In getting the deal you want, your best potential ally is your boss. Your boss will be:

- with your short-term aims, able to agree to many of them
- with your long-term aims, better placed than you are to see what the company can provide you with
- able to access the ear of higher management
- able to support you
- able to give you good advice
- most susceptible to your silent bargaining power.

Alienating your boss is unnecessary and unwise. You can alienate your boss by:

- going behind his/her back
- making threats
- grousing
- not giving your best
- not listening to his/her advice.

Because of the benefits, thrivers are always very careful to keep the boss on their side.

# Rule 15.
## Always complete.

*Don't leave a job half done. Follow your career aims through.*

There is no use leaving a job half done yet, sadly, this is what a lot of people do with career aims. Feeling the doors are closing in their faces, feeling the boss is unsympathetic, feeling they are being a nuisance are all reasons why people start to flag and give up.

Completing is important because it is the only true test of finding out whether your aims are realisable or not. Fine if they are; equally fine if they are not because now at least you know where you stand. You can decide whether:

- you dump the aim (you could try again at some point in the future)
- you modify it in some way
- you stick with the aim but try to fulfil it by going on the outside job market.

Giving up prematurely means:

*either* you go onto the outside job market unnecessarily (take a risk)

*or* you do nothing and get in a rut (an even bigger risk).

Thrivers are completers. They don't give up till they have reached a conclusion: the point where they have achieved the aim or there is nowhere further for them to go.

# Rule 16.
## Take account of risk.

*Risk is everywhere. Don't lose sight of it by pretending it doesn't exist.*

Risk is an inescapable part of corporate life and you must proceed at all times with a proper appreciation of the upsides and downsides.

Risk is at its greatest when you are promoted (or your job changes substantially for some other reason). The upside is that everything works out for you and you go on to enjoy the fruits of your changed circumstances (greater job satisfaction, more pay, elevation in your status, etc.); the downside is that you find yourself struggling or unhappy – then the challenge for you is to manage the situation as best you can.

These days careers in companies don't necessarily go in one (upwards) direction. They can take in sideways and backwards steps as well. Thrivers are people who can handle the entire range of outcomes. They work out the risks at each move. They know what to do when things don't work out.

## Rule 17.
### Face up to the reality of politics.

*Be ready to have to steer your course round conflicting interest groups. Take advantage of politics that work in your favour.*

Few companies are without politics (even small ones). In some cases these politics manifest themselves in fairly harmless and low-level bickerings. At the other end of the scale they can be vicious and extremely divisive.

The mistake with politics is to ignore them or pretend that they are not there. Politics are a reality and best dealt with by facing up to them. Sometimes they work in your favour – the fact that you are identified with a particular interest group will help to advance your career. Sometimes they work against you – an opposing interest group will attempt to stand in your way. The trick is to watch these conflicting tides and observe the way they ebb and rise. Sometimes it will pay you to drop your anchor in the sand while at other times you will be able to let yourself go with the flow.

## Rule 18.
### Never resign.

*Don't throw in the towel in a fit of pique or because you feel you can't take any more. Exits from companies should always be thought out carefully.*

Feeling unable to cope with the pressures any longer is just one reason why people resign from their jobs. Another is feeling the need to take a stand or make some kind of statement about the way the company is being run or about the way they have been treated. Resignation is usually final. Sometimes the opportunity to retract presents itself but this is by no means guaranteed.

Any sense of relief or personal satisfaction that goes with resignation is usually short-lived. Other concerns quickly crowd in – notably concerns about where the money is coming from to pay the bills.

Never resign. If you're not up to the job you've been promoted into, then this is as much the company's problem as it is yours.

If you're not happy with the way the company is going or how they are treating you, if you have not been able to resolve your misgivings or grievances by other means, take a planned and structured approach to putting yourself on the outside job market. Don't put yourself under pressure to take the first job that comes along because you no longer have a regular pay cheque coming in.

## Rule 19.
**Seek to empower yourself.**

*Chances to take on more responsibility should always be grasped. Don't put up obstacles when the authority to make decisions is delegated to you.*

Today's downsized, flattened off and slim-line world is full of opportunities to take on more responsibility. The fact that people don't take advantage of these opportunities often reflects:

- a reluctance to do so without extra pay
- the conviction in their own minds that they are 'too busy'.

Empowerment (delegation downwards of decision making authority) is a nettle you should grasp even if it does cause you a little pain. Not only will it do you good to stretch yourself, it will also add to your value and enhance your silent bargaining power.

## Rule 20.
**Be inventive and proactive.**

*See overcoming career situations as a challenge. Don't write companies off till you have pulled out all the stops.*

In the kind of career situations people find themselves in today, conventional prescriptions for achieving aims and climbing the corporate ladder don't always work. If this happens to you, the mistake is to just sit there and wait for something to happen because, nine times out of ten, it doesn't and you will still find yourself sitting there in twenty years' time.

Following a systematic approach along the lines we recommend in this book will help, but moving your career in the direction you want it to go in should always be viewed as a challenge. In this context you should never be afraid to experiment particularly with ways of enhancing your visibility.

Being proactive and taking matters into your own hands when you see a problem is all part of managing your own career. What seems like stalemate and stagnation at first sight can often be turned into something quite the opposite by the application of a little creativity.

# INDEX